You Are
LOVED

Darlene Sala

You Are
LOVED

*Inspiration to
Refresh Your Soul*

BARBOUR BOOKS
An Imprint of Barbour Publishing, Inc.

© 2014 by Darlene Sala

Readings originally published in the Philippines, under the title *Refreshing Words for Busy Women*, by OMF Literature, Inc.

Print ISBN 978-1-68322-589-8

eBook Editions:
Adobe Digital Edition (.epub) 978-1-62836-387-6
Kindle and MobiPocket Edition (.prc) 978-1-62836-388-3

Published by Barbour Books, an imprint of Barbour Publishing, Inc., 1810 Barbour Drive, Uhrichsville, Ohio 44683, www.barbourbooks.com

Our mission is to inspire the world with the life-changing message of the Bible.

Member of the
Evangelical Christian
Publishers Association

Printed in the United States of America.

DEDICATION/ACKNOWLEDGMENTS

To my husband, Harold, who never misses an opportunity to express his love for me, I dedicate this book—another opportunity to tell you that "You are loved" with all my heart. How blessed we are to serve the Lord together, depending daily on the One who loves us with an everlasting love (Jeremiah 31:3).

No book is the product of just one person. Barbour Publishing's senior editor for non-fiction, Paul Muckley, especially assisted in shaping *You Are Loved.* I am so grateful for your help, Paul, and for your confidence that encourages me to keep writing. Love is such an important part of a woman's life. When we feel loved, we function well, bouncing with the ups and downs that occur in every person's life. May your talent and effort bless the lives of those who read *this book.*

Before You Begin

"You are loved!" It's so heartwarming when someone says those words to you. You may have been at an all-time low in your life. You felt no one even cared. And then, unexpectedly, someone reached out with a hug and assured you of their love. The sky began to brighten. You actually believed you could keep going a little longer.

Have you forgotten there is someone who *always* loves you? God! The good news is that absolutely *nothing* can separate you from His love. No matter how much you goof up, no matter how you disappoint yourself, no matter how many times you fail, God's love for you never fails. How do I know? Because Romans 8:38–39 says that nothing—absolutely nothing—can separate you from the love of God. No matter the circumstances, that's His promise.

As you read the selections in this book, keep that fact firmly in mind. Oh yes, God will allow difficulties in your life—but only to strengthen you, never to hurt you. Hold on to His promises with all your heart. No matter what the circumstances, always remind yourself, *I am loved! I am loved!* God's love for you is the ultimate refreshment, giving you courage to carry on.

"I have loved you with an everlasting love."

Jeremiah 31:3

1

Then Peter came to himself and said,
"Now I know without a doubt that the Lord has
sent his angel and rescued me from Herod's
clutches and from everything the Jewish
people were hoping would happen."

ACTS 12:11
(THE WHOLE STORY: ACTS 12:1–11)

WHAT A DIFFERENCE A YEAR MAKES!

It was Passover, and the apostle Peter was in prison sleeping between two soldiers, bound with chains, with sentries standing guard. No Passover meal for Peter.

Where had Peter celebrated the previous Passover just a year ago? At that unforgettable meal with Jesus, the Last Supper. In prison, Peter had all the time in the world to remember.

He must have remembered that Jesus washed his feet that night. Remembered that he told Jesus he would rather die than deny Him. With what shame he must have remembered that three times he denied that he even knew Him—then wept bitterly.

The crucifixion followed, and afterward Jesus' body was put in a tomb. But then came Resurrection Day! Peter saw for himself that the tomb was empty. There was that thrilling moment when Jesus appeared in front of him and the other disciples. Later the risen Savior ate breakfast with them on the shores of Galilee and Jesus told Peter, "Follow Me" (John 21:22).

Peter's trial was to be very soon (Acts 12:4). He might shortly suffer the same fate as his Lord. Now in prison waiting for the outcome, Peter had the peace of knowing he had been obedient and that his life was in God's hands. And so he slept soundly—even in prison.

Later, after his miraculous release, he wrote: "In all this you greatly rejoice, though now for a little while you may have had to suffer grief in all kinds of trials" (1 Peter 1:6). "Cast all your anxiety on him because he cares for you" (1 Peter 5:7).

Like Peter, may we too obey Jesus' command: "Follow Me."

2

*When Jesus spoke again to the people,
he said, "I am the light of the world.
Whoever follows me will never walk in
darkness, but will have the light of life."*

JOHN 8:12

GOD INTERVENES

At the age of ten my dad dedicated his life to serve the Lord, and longed to go to Bible college. His parents, however, thought he should go to a secular college.

One day toward the end of his senior year of high school he was standing waist deep in a swimming pool during physical education class. My dad felt a strange sensation and began to lose consciousness. He remembered praying, "Lord, save me!" as he slipped under the water. An alert lifeguard saw him lying at the bottom of the pool and rescued him.

In June of the following year, he fell unconscious again. There was no logical explanation for either incident, but a day or so later, his mother greeted him as he arrived home, tears streaming down her face. Throwing her arms around him, she said the Lord showed her that these incidents had occurred because she wanted him to go to secular college. She said, "You can go to Bible school tomorrow if you want to."

When the fall semester began, you can be sure that my dad was on the front row of the student assembly at Bible school. For the remaining seventy-four years of his life, he faithfully served the Lord as an evangelist, pastor, author, and seminary professor.

Incidentally, my dad was never unconscious again in his entire life of eighty-nine years. His favorite Bible verse when it came to guidance for life was John 8:12, where Jesus said: "I am the light of the world. Whoever follows me will never walk in darkness, but will have the light of life." How wonderful to have a God who personally directs our lives!

3

By the word of the LORD the heavens were made,
their starry host by the breath of his mouth.

PSALM 33:6

BIGGER THAN THE SOMBRERO GALAXY

One of the most beautiful galaxies viewable from earth is the Sombrero Galaxy. This brilliant heavenly mass got its interesting name from its resemblance to a broad-rimmed Mexican hat. Even though this galaxy is just beyond what the naked eye can see, data from the Hubble Telescope has determined that it's actually a massive object equivalent to eight hundred billion suns. If you were to travel from one side to the other of the Sombrero Galaxy, it would take you fifty thousand light years![1]

Our minds have trouble wrapping themselves around anything of such large dimensions. But even if we can't truly grasp how massive eight hundred billion suns are, just trying to understand is good for us because the effort enlarges our concept of how big God is. If God made the heavens, He must be bigger than, greater than, and superior to anything He has made, right? Does it not follow, then, that He must be bigger than our problems?

"By the word of the Lord the heavens were made, their starry host by the breath of his mouth" (Psalm 33:6). *Poof!* Just like that God created our tremendous heavens and earth! Even a glimpse of how big our God is makes trusting Him easier.

Check out a book on astronomy. If you have access to the internet, search the size of the universe. Investigate the heavens, and I can pretty well guarantee that your faith in God will grow.

¹ http://hubblesite.org/newscenter/archive/releases/2003/28/image/a/,accessed September 17, 2008

4

Give thanks in all circumstances;
for this is God's will for you in Christ Jesus.

1 THESSALONIANS 5:18

THE HAT

"When I became pastor of my first church in Canada," related my dad, "I noticed that virtually every man wore a hat. So I decided that if I wanted to be a respectable member of Canadian society, I should purchase a hat—and I did: a beautiful, light tan fedora.

"After about two years, I noticed that my hat had become terribly dirty, and I began to pray for the money to get it cleaned. Somehow I managed to get seventy-five cents together, and had my hat cleaned.

"The next Monday night I wore my hat to church for what we called a fellowship service—a specially blessed time. I was praising the Lord as I walked home—when all of a sudden, the most cantankerous wind came and lifted my beautiful, clean hat off my head and deposited it in a mud puddle.

"Resentment welled up and the blessedness I felt quickly leaked out. As I picked up my hat, I fully expected to see the underside completely muddy. But as I turned it over, to my amazement there was just one little piece of dirt. I flicked it off with my finger and it was gone.

"I said, 'Why, you dirty old devil. You almost robbed me of a great blessing over absolutely nothing.' I put my hat on my head and walked home with joy."

Then Dad concluded, "Whatever you do, do not allow some petty annoyance to rob you of the sweetness of God's blessing in your life."

As the apostle Paul said, "Give thanks in all circumstances, for this is God's will for you in Christ Jesus" (1 Thessalonians 5:18).

5

Yet I Will Rejoice

The prophet Habakkuk lived in a day of uncertainty. Babylon was growing as a world power, and the people of Judah were afraid for their lives. Yet for all his questions about the future, the prophet ends his writings with a song of encouragement that confidently declares that God will protect and sustain His people. He writes,

> *Though the fig tree does not bud*
> *and there are no grapes on the vines,*
> *though the olive crop fails*
> *and the fields produce no food,*
> *though there are no sheep in the pen*
> *and no cattle in the stalls,*
> *yet I will rejoice in the LORD,*
> *I will be joyful in God my Savior.*
> HABAKKUK 3:17–18

If Habakkuk were writing today, he would have written something like this:

Though the Gross National Product does not rise,
and there is no pay increase this year,
though the stock market falls
and retirement benefits end,
though negotiations be broken off
and there be no hope of peace in the world,
yet I will rejoice in the Lord,
I will be joyful in God my Savior.

I have homework for you today. Before you go to sleep tonight, please open your Bible, read Habakkuk, and write your own paraphrase of the last verses of this book. Substitute your problems for Habakkuk's. When you get to the part where Habakkuk says he will still be joyful and rejoice in the Lord in spite of all the problems, tell God the same. I believe you will be encouraged.

6

Oh, the depth of the riches of
the wisdom and knowledge of God!
How unsearchable his judgments,
and his paths beyond tracing out!

ROMANS 11:33

THE OWNER OF THE BIBLE

The following is a true story told by Bill Bright, founder of Campus Crusade for Christ.

In the 1930s, Stalin ordered a purge of all Bibles in the former Soviet Union. He had millions of Bibles confiscated. In Stavropol, Russia, this order was carried out with a vengeance.

A few years ago, a missions team was sent to Stavropol. When the team couldn't get Bibles from Moscow, someone mentioned that the Bibles confiscated in Stalin's days had been stored in a warehouse outside of town.

One member finally got up the courage to ask government officials if the Bibles were still there and could be distributed to the people. The answer was "Yes"!

The missions team arrived at the warehouse with a truck and a young Russian who was hired to help load the Bibles. A hostile, skeptical, agnostic collegian, he had come only for the day's wages.

As the team was loading the Bibles, the young man disappeared. Eventually, they saw him in a corner of the warehouse, weeping. He had slipped away hoping to quietly take a Bible. What he found shook him. Inside the Bible he had picked up was the handwritten signature of his grandmother! Out of the many thousands of Bibles in the warehouse, he had stolen the one belonging to her. She had no doubt prayed for him, and now this young man's life was being transformed by the very Bible that his grandmother found so dear.

"Oh, the depth of the riches of the wisdom and knowledge of God!" the Bible says, "How unsearchable his judgments, and his paths beyond tracing out" (Romans 11:33). In His wisdom He answers our prayers with perfect timing.

7

For the LORD God is a sun and shield;
the LORD bestows favor and honor;
no good thing does he withhold
from those whose walk is blameless.

PSALM 84:11

MAKING BEAUTIFUL MUSIC

When a composer visited the cathedral at Friedberg, Germany, he heard the magnificent sounds of the great organ there. Climbing up to the loft, he asked permission to play it. The old organist refused but was finally persuaded. After listening with delight and amazement to the glorious music, the old man laid his hand on the shoulder of the inspired musician and exclaimed, "Who are you? What is your name?"

"Felix Mendelssohn," replied the player.

Like the organist, control can be such an issue for us. How many of us let God, the Master Musician of the universe, have full access to the keyboard of our lives? Often we hesitate to get off the organ bench and let Him compose our life's music.

When will we learn that God wants only the best for us? The Bible is full of verses that tell us this:

- No good thing will he withhold from them that walk uprightly (Psalm 84:11 KJV).

- Every good and perfect gift is from above, coming down from the Father of the heavenly lights, who does not change like shifting shadows (James 1:17).

- Those who seek the LORD lack no good thing (Psalm 34:10).

- "If you, then, though you are evil, know how to give good gifts to your children, how much more will your Father in heaven give good gifts to those who ask him!" (Matthew 7:11).

With promises like these, how can we afford to run our own lives? We'd be fools to try. Get off the organ bench and listen to the beautiful music God will make out of your life.

8

I will extol the LORD at all times;
his praise will always be on my lips.

PSALM 34:1

AT ALL TIMES AND IN ALL PLACES, GIVE THANKS

Author Elizabeth Sherrill was frustrated. Having flown in to speak at a seminar for Christian writers, she was annoyed that part of her luggage had not arrived, including her dress shoes.

"Of *all times* for this to happen," she said to herself. Then a phrase came to her mind: "We should at all times and in all places, give thanks unto Thee."

So Elizabeth went ahead with her session. At the end of the seminar, several writers came up to the platform. Suddenly there was the sound of gunfire and breaking glass. A woman shouted, "Lie down everyone!"

Outside two drunk men were taking potshots at telephone poles. One of the shots had come through a window, and the "bullet," which was the tip of an electric screwdriver shot from a homemade gun, lodged in the wall behind the speaker's stand.

As police reports were being filled out, Elizabeth traced the trajectory of the bullet from the window to its resting place, just one inch above her head. Her mind went immediately to a pair of shoes with two-and-a-half-inch heels in a missing suitcase and a prayer, "We should at all times and in all places, give thanks unto Thee, O Lord."[1]

How many times have we come close to death and not even realized it? A car accident that didn't happen. An armed robbery that God prevented. On an occasion when King David had just experienced one of his many close calls with death, he said, "I will extol the LORD at all times; his praise will always be on my lips" (Psalm 34:1). Let's remember to give thanks to the Lord at all times and in all places.

---

[1]Elizabeth Sherrill, "The Missing Shoe," in *His Mysterious Ways,* vol. 2 (Carmel, NY: Guideposts Associates, Inc., 1991), 46–47.

9

Who is a God like you, who pardons sin and forgives the transgression of the remnant of his inheritance? You do not stay angry forever but delight to show mercy. You will again have compassion on us; you will tread our sins underfoot and hurl all our iniquities into the depths of the sea.

MICAH 7:18–19

WHAT GOD DOES WITH OUR SINS

Have you just done something you know you shouldn't have done? Are you afraid God will never forgive you for it? Then read these encouraging verses written by the Old Testament prophet Micah: "Who is a God like you, who pardons sin and forgives the transgression. . . ? You do not stay angry forever but delight to show mercy. You will again have compassion on us; you will tread our sins underfoot and hurl all our iniquities into the depths of the sea" (Micah 7:18–19).

I love the word pictures Micah used. He said that God, in His compassion, grinds our sins into the ground under His great foot. As you would step on a poisonous spider so that you would never have to deal with it again, God tramples our sins underfoot.

In the next word picture, Micah said God hurls all our sins into the depths of the sea. Notice that God doesn't deposit them near the shoreline, where they might be washed ashore with the tide. Nor does He merely drop them into the sea. No, He *hurls* them. And then, as Corrie ten Boom said, He puts up a sign that says, "No Fishing."

Other verses in the Bible tell us that God sweeps away our sins like the morning mist that evaporates so quickly (Isaiah 44:22)—that He blots out our sins and remembers them no more (Isaiah 43:25).

That thing you know you shouldn't have done? Admit right now that you did wrong and ask God to forgive you. Then watch as He hurls your sin into the deepest sea.

10

"Here I am! I stand at the door and knock.
If anyone hears my voice and opens the door,
I will come in and eat with that person,
and they with me."

REVELATION 3:20

THE PRISON WALLS OF LONELINESS

Can you imagine being in solitary confinement for years? That was the experience of Madame Jeanne Guyon, a French mystic in the seventeenth century. Madame Guyon was imprisoned in the infamous Paris Bastille for her belief that anyone can directly enjoy God's presence through constant, reflective, and intimate prayer. Madame Guyon was in prison but her attitude made all the difference. She believed that she was there in the will of God. The reality that God was with her helped her survive the terrible living conditions.

She learned that moment-by-moment communication with God banishes loneliness. Madame Guyon chose to accept thing that happened to her as from the hand of God. She learned not to fight difficulties but to live with them, believing that since God allowed them, He would supply the strength she needed. She had such great delight in God that her spirit soared far above the prison walls. In fact, she said the stones in her prison shone like rubies. She wrote,

> *A little bird am I.*
> *Shut out from fields of air,*
> *Yet in my cage I sit and sing*
> *To him who placed me there!*
> *Well pleased a prisoner to be,*
> *Because, my God, it pleaseth Thee.*[1]

Are you feeling isolated and alone? Jesus said, "Here I am! I stand at the door and knock. If anyone hears my voice and opens the door, I will come in and eat with that person, and they with me" (Revelation 3:20). When you make Him your dearest friend, you too can soar above the prison walls of loneliness.

---

[1] http://www.cowart.info/John's%20Books/Guyon/Guyon.htm, accessed September 9, 2008.

11

I am not saying this because I am in need, for I have learned to be content whatever the circumstances. I know what it is to be in need, and I know what it is to have plenty. I have learned the secret of being content in any and every situation, whether well fed or hungry, whether living in plenty or in want.

PHILIPPIANS 4:11–12

contentment

Author Linda Dillow writes about a young bride who married a marine, thinking that traveling the globe and living in foreign countries would be romantic and exciting. Two years later, she wrote her complaints to her mother. She said she had no friends. Worst of all, her husband was never home. She wrote, "I can't take this any longer. I'm coming home." Her wise mother's short reply:

Two women looked through prison bars
One saw mud, the other saw stars.[1]

Each of us has a choice. As Linda writes,

Every woman has circumstances that appear to be prison bars. God wants you and me to learn to be content in our circumstances, not when they improve.[2]

Linda's observation follows the apostle Paul's example. He wrote, "I have learned to be content whatever the circumstances. I know what it is to be in need, and I know what it is to have plenty. I have learned the secret of being content in any and every situation" (Philippians 4:11–12).

Paul "learned" to be content. Mary Southerland says that "learned" means "to be educated by experience."[3]

Contentment is difficult to learn, but not impossible. The Bible teaches us: "In every situation, by prayer and petition, with thanksgiving, present your requests to God. And the peace of God, which transcends all understanding, will guard your hearts and your minds in Christ Jesus" (Philippians 4:6–7). That's how we learn contentment: we pray—and find God's peace.

[1]Linda Dillow, *Calm My Anxious Heart* (Colorado Springs, CO: NavPress, 1998), 25–26.
[2]Ibid., 26.
[3]Mary Southerland, *Experiencing God's Power in Your Ministry* (Eugene, OR: Harvest House Publishers, 2006), 153.

12

The disciples went and woke him, saying, "Master, Master, we're going to drown!" He got up and rebuked the wind and the raging waters; the storm subsided, and all was calm.

LUKE 8:24

(THE WHOLE STORY: LUKE 8:22–25)

THE STORM CAN'T SINK US

Liz was a new Christian who had been attending my Bible study group for several weeks. Although she hadn't had a relationship with Jesus Christ for very long, she contributed much to our discussions. Often she amazed me with her insights into scripture.

One week we were studying the incident in Luke 8 where some of the disciples were in a boat with Jesus, crossing the Sea of Galilee at night. When a sudden storm came up, Jesus was asleep in the boat. The disciples roused Him, asking, "Master, don't You care that we're sinking?" Jesus rebuked the storm, and immediately the sea was calm.

Our discussion question was, "Think about the most difficult situation you now face. What phrase in this passage brings comfort to you?" Most people in the group agreed that it was verse 24, where Jesus "rebuked the wind and the raging waters; the storm subsided, and all was calm." But Liz said that the part she liked best was when Jesus fell asleep. Curious, I asked why.

She replied, "Sometimes we feel God is asleep at the wheel of our lives—we can't sense Him doing anything about our problems. But His presence with us is enough. Whether we see Him doing anything about the storm or not, we know that when He is with us, the storm can't sink us!"

Do you have that confidence? If you have invited Jesus to be Lord of your life, He will be with you in the inevitable storms you'll experience. You can't sink when Jesus is in your boat.

13

Then I heard a loud voice in heaven say: "Now have come the salvation and the power and the kingdom of our God, and the authority of his Messiah. For the accuser of our brothers and sisters, who accuses them before our God day and night, has been hurled down."

REVELATION 12:10

CONFESSING TO THE DEVIL

Does the following describe you? You know you've done something that God isn't happy about—let's be honest, it's sin. You also know that Christ died for your sins. So you've confessed this sin to God, and He has forgiven you, for the Bible says, "If we confess our sins, he is faithful and just and will forgive us our sins" (1 John 1:9). That clears your conscience, right?

Well, maybe not. When you open your eyes the next morning, possibly you still have nagging feelings of guilt. You don't *feel* forgiven. So you confess your sin and ask God to forgive you all over again. It becomes an ever-repeating cycle.

My dad, who was a minister, believed that it is the devil that makes us feel guilty for sins already forgiven because he lies to us. He is called "the accuser of our brothers and sisters, who accuses them before our God day and night" (Revelation 12:10). The apostle John tells us how Jesus described the devil: "When he lies, he speaks his native language, for he is a liar and the father of lies" (John 8:44).

When God has forgiven you, He has forgotten your sins. He is not your accuser. The Bible says, "There is now no condemnation for those who are in Christ Jesus" (Romans 8:1). Who else is left to accuse us? Only the devil.

But there's good news. The Bible says that we can "demolish arguments and every pretension that sets itself up against the knowledge of God, and we take captive every thought to make it obedient to Christ" (2 Corinthians 10:5). Resist the devil's lies and accept the truth of God's forgiveness. Then joy will replace your feelings of guilt.

14

"His eyes are on the ways of mortals;
he sees their every step."

Job 34:21

GOD KNOWS EXACTLY WHERE YOU ARE

When our son became serious about rock climbing and backcountry skiing, we, his parents, became very serious about doing all we could to ensure his safety. We bought him a GPS unit, a small handheld device that tells him his location.

GPS stands for Global Positioning System, a space-based radio navigation system consisting of satellites and a network of ground stations for monitoring and control. A minimum of twenty-four GPS satellites orbit the earth at an altitude of approximately eleven thousand miles. These provide users with accurate information on their location anywhere in the world, in all weather conditions.

In practical terms, this means that when my son begins one of his adventures, he can set the GPS unit to record his starting location. He can then always find his way back, for the GPS unit tells him exactly where he is and guides him back to his starting point.

God must smile at our scientific inventions—simple toys to Him who has all knowledge. The Bible says, "From heaven the LORD looks down and sees all mankind" (Psalm 33:13). "His eyes are on the ways of mortals; he sees their every step" (Job 34:21).

How wonderful to know that God *always* knows where we are. As helpful as a GPS unit is, if the battery inside does not work, the unit is worthless. But God is always aware of our exact location. The Bible says, "The LORD watches over all who love him" (Psalm 145:20), and "The LORD will guide you always" (Isaiah 58:11).

Let those promises reassure you.

15

*"Everyone who calls on the
name of the Lord will be saved."*

ROMANS 10:13

180-DEGREE CHANGE

An English earl who was visiting the Fiji Islands remarked to an elderly chief, "You're a great leader, but it's a pity you've been taken in by those foreign missionaries. They only want to get rich through you. No one believes the Bible anymore."

The old chief's eyes flashed. "See that great rock over there? On it we smashed the heads of our victims. Notice the furnace next to it? In that oven we roasted their bodies. If it hadn't been for those good missionaries and the love of Jesus that changed us from cannibals into Christians, you'd never leave this place alive! You'd better thank the Lord for the Gospel."[1]

Today God still changes lives 180 degrees! Roy was hooked on alcohol and drugs, and nearly died. Desperate, he was ready to try anything to get out of the pit he was in.

His younger sister went to church, so he asked her if maybe church would change him. She called an evangelist who told Roy how to accept Jesus as his Savior. Roy thought, *What have I got to lose?* and prayed for Jesus to come into his life.

The next morning he awoke, overflowing with love and joy. When he told his girlfriend he had no desire to drink or take drugs anymore, she said, "You couldn't have changed like this overnight. You're faking it!"

"You're right, I couldn't," he said, "but God changed me!" Roy adds, "You're never too far gone for God to forgive you and change your life. I know!"[2]

Romans 10:13 says, "Everyone who calls on the name of the Lord will be saved." Maybe you're ready for a 180-degree change! Let God transform you.

---

[1]M. R. DeHaan, "The Wonderful Change," *Our Daily Bread,* (Grand Rapids, MI: Radio Bible Class, 1972).
[2]http://www.webspawner.com/users/royecork/, accessed September 15, 2008

16

Each of you should use whatever gift
you have received to serve others, as faithful
stewards of God's grace in its various forms.

1 PETER 4:10

A FRIEND WHO INSPIRES ME

Some people are an inspiration—just thinking about them encourages you when the going is tough. Loana is such a friend. She has always been a joy to know, a faithful wife and mother of five. But when her husband died and she had to pick up the pieces of life and go on, I saw a depth in her that I had not known before.

Music has always been a big part of Loana's life. When her kids were young, the whole family sang together. She is one of the best piano accompanists I know, and she often accompanied her husband, Jim, when he sang in his rich tenor voice.

For years Loana and Jim had a Christmas tradition of inviting friends to their home for a carol sing-along, accompanied by great food. But after Jim died, she couldn't bring herself to do it. The memories were just too painful. Then one Christmas, I received an unexpected invitation to come to her home.

The house was fully decorated for Christmas, and beautiful china and crystal adorned the table. I had thought that we'd be eating a few snacks that evening, but Loana had prepared a delicious full dinner for us. Afterward, she sat down at the piano and led us in singing all our favorite carols.

The whole evening was special because of the gift that Loana gave to each of us—the gift of herself. The apostle Peter said, "Each of you should use whatever gift you have received to serve others, faithful stewards of God's grace in its various forms" (1 Peter 4:10).

Thank you, Loana. You've done just that.

17

*When I saw him, I fell at his feet as though dead. Then he placed
his right hand on me and said: "Do not be afraid. I am the
First and the Last. I am the Living One; I was dead,
and now look, I am alive for ever and ever!
And I hold the keys of death and Hades."*

REVELATION 1:17–18

THE BEGINNING, THE END,
AND EVERYTHING IN BETWEEN

In the last book of the Bible, Revelation, Jesus says, "Do not be
afraid. I am the First and the Last. I am the Living One; I was dead,
and now look, I am alive for ever and ever!" (Revelation 1:17–18).

I was privileged to grow up knowing that God was the
beginning of everything. I learned early that there is nothing
that predates God. He was and is the First. As I've gotten older,
I'm glad to know that He is also the Last—nothing will ever
come after Him. Another Bible translation, the King James
Version, says He is Alpha and Omega—the first and last letters
of the Greek alphabet.

God was there for my beginning years, bringing me through a difficult birth and a serious childhood infection. And I'm so glad to know He will be there for the ending years of my life as well.

Eventually there comes a time when your birthday seems to come around faster and faster, and the years begin to add up. You realize you've hit the peak of your career. You develop health problems. You wonder what the rest of your life holds. Be encouraged by remembering that Jesus is Alpha and Omega, the beginning *and* the end. He has a plan for your later years just as much as He did in your early years.

Whatever period of life you are in, Jesus is there for you. While it's true that He is Alpha and Omega, He is also all the letters in between. He wants to be your whole alphabet. Aren't you glad!

18

For you know the grace of our Lord Jesus Christ,
that though he was rich, yet for your sake he became poor,
so that you through his poverty might become rich.

2 CORINTHIANS 8:9

grace

❧ ✿ ❧

The apostle Paul so often began his writings to the New Testament churches with the greetings "Grace and peace." Bible teacher G. Campbell Morgan says that in the Greek language, *grace* was, first of all, an intellectual and artistic word. It included the idea of "beauty as against ugliness, health as against disease, order as against chaos, all the realm of that which is beautiful."[1]

In time the word came to mean God's desire to impart order and beauty and life to us—a giving. A fuller meaning of grace, however, includes not merely the gifts and the desire to give those gifts, but also the activity that carries out the desire. "Grace," writes Morgan, "is ultimately the activity of God which puts at the disposal of sinful men and women all the things that give delight to Him."[2]

When a baby is born, the parents look at their little one and anticipate all the wonderful experiences they want to share with their child. Because they love their baby, they can hardly wait to give to him out of the joy in their hearts.

Is God so different? Out of His heart of love, He has made us spiritually rich. "For you know the grace of our Lord Jesus Christ," wrote Paul, "that though he was rich, yet for your sake he became poor, so that you through his poverty might become rich" (2 Corinthians 8:9).

God's grace! We don't deserve it. Today, stop and say, "Thank You, Lord!"

[1]G. Campbell Morgan, *The Corinthian Letters of Paul* (New York: Fleming H. Revell Company, 1946), 14.
[2]Ibid.

19

*"His master replied, 'Well done, good and faithful servant!
You have been faithful with a few things; I will put you in
charge of many things. Come and share your master's happiness!' "*

MATTHEW 25:23

IF I JUST HAD ENOUGH MONEY

Finish this statement: "If I just had enough money, I would..." Would you change your lifestyle? Help stop HIV/AIDS? Relieve world hunger? Share the Gospel in massive ways?

I'm sure that some of the things we'd do if we had enough money would be selfish, while other things would make a tremendous difference in our world. Watching the news on TV, you may feel overwhelmed by the needs and suffering of so many. But God holds us responsible only for what we can do.

My husband tells the story about two boys who were walking along a beach where an unusually high tide had washed a lot of crabs onto the shore. If the crabs were not soon returned to the water, they could die. One of the boys started picking up crabs and hurling them back into the ocean as fast as he could. His friend said, "Why are you doing that? You can't save them all."

"No, I can't," replied the first boy, "but it makes a tremendous difference for the ones I do save."

When I was a kid I heard a little rhyme that stuck with me:

It's not what you'd do with money,
if riches should be your lot.
It's what you're already doing with
the dollar-and-a-quarter you've got.

You and I have enough money to do whatever it is that God wants us to do, and what we do makes a difference for those we help. May we do what we can so that one day, we can hear the Master's words, "Well done, good and faithful servant!" (Matthew 25:23).

20

Love is patient, love is kind. . . . Love never fails.

1 CORINTHIANS 13:4, 8
(THE WHOLE STORY: 1 CORINTHIANS 13:4–8)

TRUE LOVE

I read the following on a wall plaque in a restaurant:

Love puts the fun in together,
The sad in apart,
The hope in tomorrow,
The joy in a heart.

I like that. It's true that love gives us joy in being together. When we can't be together with the ones we love, we're sad, for love always desires closeness. What exactly is love? It's hard to define, isn't it? More than just an emotion or passion, love is a commitment to care.

When two single people are attracted to each other, a spark ignites their relationship. This may be intense at first, but it can't truly be called love yet because they still don't know each other deeply. As they spend time together sharing their innermost selves, the attraction grows. They discover respect for each other's ideas, common life goals, and an ever-growing desire to spend the rest of their lives together.

More than the warm, happy feelings love gives us, love also drives us to sacrifice for each other. True love is unselfish. In fact, if you want a description of true love, you can do no better than that famous chapter in the Bible, 1 Corinthians 13. It says,

Love is patient and kind. Love is not jealous or boastful or proud or rude. It does not demand its own way. It is not irritable, and it keeps no record of being wronged. It does not rejoice about injustice but rejoices whenever the truth wins out. Love never gives up, never loses faith, is always hopeful, and endures through every circumstance. Prophecy and speaking in unknown languages and special knowledge will become useless. But love will last forever!
1 Corinthians 13:4–8 nlt

Now, *that's* true love.

21

*"Now this is eternal life: that they know you,
the only true God, and Jesus Christ, whom you have sent."*

JOHN 17:3

WHAT ARE BLESSINGS?

Larry Crabb, author and psychologist, tells of the time when the doctor told him they had found a mass the size of a tennis ball near his stomach; it was likely malignant.

From his hospital window that evening he noticed a Starbucks café across the street. He imagined a Christian couple there sipping decaf lattés before they would drive home, snuggle in bed, and then get up the next morning for church. He thought, *They have the abundant life; I have cancer. It's not fair.*

Then God spoke to his heart. Larry shared,

I was more aware of my desires for health and good times. My eyes focused. I realized that I wanted God more than anything or anyone else, with my whole being. . . . That night I experienced the presence of God. What more—or less—could I want?[1]

We think we're closest to God when everything is going well — that smooth sailing in our lives is a sign of God's blessing. What are God's blessings? Health? Good times? Have we lost sight of the fact that, as Larry discovered, the greatest blessing is knowing God? Larry said,

> *Every hard thing we endure can put us in touch with our desire for God, and every trial can strengthen that desire until it becomes the consuming passion of our life. Then comes the experience of God. . . . It's the source of our deepest joy, the real point of living.*[2]

Friend, if you still do not know God, "the source of our deepest joy" and "the real point of living," I pray that you will turn to Him. "Now this is eternal life: that [you] know. . .the only true God, and Jesus Christ, whom [God] sent" (John 17:3). Knowing Him is truly the greatest blessing of our lives.

---

[1]Larry Crabb, "When Life Begins," *Spirit of Revival* (Buchanan, MI: Life Action Ministries, Volume 36, Number 1), 4–6.
[2]Ibid.

22

I desire to depart and be with Christ,
which is better by far.

PHILIPPIANS 1:23
(THE WHOLE STORY: PHILIPPIANS 1:20–24)

WHAT YOU HAVE TO BE TO GET THERE

A pastor was talking to a group of children about going to heaven. He asked, "Where do you want to go?"

"Heaven!" they all piped up.

Again, the pastor asked, "And what do you have to be to get there?"

"Dead!" one boy yelled.[1]

You'd think we didn't want to go to heaven, the way we fight death and aging. Searching for the fountain of eternal youth, we seem to begrudge every grain of sand that passes through the hourglass of life. The apostle Paul's outlook was such a contrast to this attitude. His desire was that Christ would be exalted in his body, as he put it, "whether by life or by death. For to me, to live is Christ and to die is gain. . . . Yet what shall I choose? I do not know! I am torn between the two: I desire to depart and be with Christ, which is better by far" (Philippians 1:20–23).

Paul did not dread death because, as he wrote, "We . . . know that as long as we are at home in the body we are away from the Lord. . . . We are confident, I say, and would prefer to be away from the body and at home with the Lord" (2 Corinthians 5:6, 8).

Can you be sure that if you die today you'll go to heaven? You can. Because Jesus rose from the grave, we know that He has conquered death. As you ask for forgiveness for your sins and commit your life to Him, you will receive the confidence that Paul had. You can look forward to heaven. What a destination!

[1]Stan Toler, *Humor for a Mom's Heart* (West Monroe, LA: Howard Publishing Company, 2002), 166.

23

And not only that, but we also glory in tribulations,
knowing that tribulation produces perseverance.

ROMANS 5:3 NKJV

OLD WORD, BUT UP-TO-DATE PROBLEM

Tribulation is a word that you probably don't use often, but you experience it nearly every day. Tribulation means trouble, problems, hardship, misery, difficulty, distress, ordeals, pain, and suffering.

You may think, *I'm an expert in tribulation!* Then you'll be interested in the origin of the word. When Rome ruled the world, grain was a precious commodity. Across the sheaves of cut grain, the Romans pulled a cart that had rollers instead of wheels. Sharp stones and rough bits of iron were attached to these rollers to separate the husks from the grain. This cart was called a *tribulum*. From *tribulum* we got our word "tribulation"—a fitting expression for how troubles grind us and put us under pressure.

A Roman farmer, however, did not use his *tribulum* to destroy grain—only to refine it. God also uses our troubles to make us stronger, for "tribulation produces perseverance" (Romans 5:3 NKJV).

The apostle Paul wrote that God "comforts us in all our tribulation" (2 Corinthians 1:4 NKJV). "Comfort" and "tribulation" go together. When we experience tribulation, we desperately need someone who will comfort us. How fortunate we are that we have the Holy Spirit, the Comforter (John 14:26 KJV).

Bible teacher G. Campbell Morgan says that *comfort* means more than reassurance or consolation. It is also reinforcing a person and sustaining him; it is coming to his side to help. God's comfort is no less than His strengthening companionship and upholding power.[1]

Experiencing tribulation? Ask God's help. The divine Comforter will strengthen you.

[1] G. Campbell Morgan, *The Corinthian Letters of Paul* (New York: Fleming H. Revell Company, 1946), 227.

24

We love because he first loved us.

1 JOHN 4:19

TELLING GOD "I LOVE YOU"

Dr. Gary Chapman says there are five "Love Languages." Love languages are ways we express love, whether to a spouse, a child, family, or friends. They are the languages of gifts, touch, acts of service, words, and quality time. Each of us has a primary love language that we use and respond to.

I believe these five love languages are also ways through which we can express love to our heavenly Father. Let's see how.

First, we can express love to God through gifts, such as a portion of our money. Love is to be the motive for all that we give to Him. Remember: God so loved us that He gave us His Son.

When it comes to touch, while we can't physically touch God, we can certainly touch Him in quiet, concentrated prayer.

An act of service for others is also a way of expressing love for God, for when we show kindness to people, Jesus said we're actually doing it to Him (Matthew 25:31–46).

What about words? It's easy to think, *Well, God knows everything, so He already knows I love Him. I don't need to tell Him.* But God longs to hear us say we love Him.

Then there's quality time. This is not just time for prayer; it is focusing our thoughts on God throughout the day. Thomas Merton, a Trappist monk, wrote: "Solitude is not turning one's back on the world; it is turning our face toward God."[1]

Have you expressed your love to God today? You have five ways to do it. John wrote, "We love because he first loved us" (1 John 4:19).

[1]Thomas Merton, *New Seeds of Contemplation* (New York: New Directions, 1962), 52–63.

25

For everything that was written in the past was written to teach us, so that through the endurance taught in the Scriptures and the encouragement they provide we might have hope. May the God who gives endurance and encouragement give you the same attitude of mind toward each other that Christ Jesus had.

ROMANS 15:4–5

THE GOD WHO GIVES
ENDURANCE AND ENCOURAGEMENT

I like to read the bestseller list to see what kinds of books people are buying. Many are fiction. Most deal with various issues of life in the twenty-first century. But there's one book on the best-seller list that dates back more than four thousand years—yet people still read it today. Of course, it's the Bible. Amazing, isn't it, that people still read a book that was written so many years ago!

Most of us tend to read the New Testament more than we do the Old Testament. Some reason, "Why bother to read the Old Testament? Wasn't it replaced by the teachings of Jesus?" The Bible itself tells us why to bother. In the book of Romans, Paul wrote, "For everything that was written in the past was written to teach us, so that through the endurance taught in the Scriptures and the encouragement they provide we might have hope" (Romans 15:4). The next verse calls God "the God who gives endurance and encouragement."

You see, when we read the Old Testament we learn principles about God—about His character and how He deals with us human beings. Because the writing of the Old Testament covered a period of about 1,400 years, we see God's faithfulness over a long period of time. Over the centuries He kept His promises. He supplied the needs of His people. What He said would happen came true. This encourages us to keep trusting God with our problems.

Need a fresh injection of hope today? For a change, read the Old Testament. Perhaps Isaiah 41 would be an interesting place to start. You will see the God who gives endurance and encouragement (Romans 15:5)—and hope.

26

Whoever dwells in the shelter of the Most High will rest in the shadow of the Almighty. I will say of the LORD, "He is my refuge and my fortress, my God, in whom I trust." Surely he will save you from the fowler's snare and from the deadly pestilence. He will cover you with his feathers, and under his wings you will find refuge; his faithfulness will be your shield and rampart.

PSALM 91:1–4

Dark Days

I'm always fascinated to listen to people tell how God met them at a point of desperation. Take the Elegados, for instance. In the mining business during the Japanese occupation of the Philippines, Mr. Elegado had the only car allowed to enter sensitive areas; to pass checkpoints he had to have a Japanese sticker on the car.

Eventually, however, he was arrested by the Japanese and taken to prison. For months his wife left their children every weekend to search for him. She knew that if she did not find him he would die, for he could not survive on prison rations.

Her heart cried out, "If there is a God—if You are really alive—help me."

At the end of eight months of searching, she found him and began to bring food to him. God preserved his life through two more years of imprisonment in that dark place, and ever since that time she and her husband have been dedicated to the Lord.

There is a postscript to the story. The Japanese imprisonment, horrible as it was, saved Mr. Elegado's life. For immediately after he was arrested, the Filipino guerrillas sought to kill him for the Japanese sticker on his car. But Mr. Elegado was safe in prison.

When we are in a very dark place, perhaps the darkness is only the shadow of God's hand shielding us from greater danger. Psalm 91 says, "He who dwells in the shelter of the Most High will rest in the shadow of the Almighty. . . . He will cover you with his feathers, and under his wings you will find refuge" (verses 1 and 4).

27

*Then God said, "Let us make mankind in our image,
in our likeness, so that they may rule over the fish in the sea and
the birds in the sky, over the livestock and all the wild animals,
and over all the creatures that move along the ground."
So God created mankind in his own image, in the image of
God he created them; male and female he created them.*

Genesis 1:26–27

image

Image is so important to a woman. Our appearance and the impression we make certainly extend the time we spend in front of the mirror beyond that of our male family members!

We want to know what the "look" is for this season so we can have the "correct image." Should our shoes match our purse? What makeup will do wonders?

Now, we do feel better about ourselves when we look nice. Part of our self-esteem may come from our appearance, but I'm quick to say it's a pretty superficial kind of self-esteem.

Image is talked about in the Bible too—but it's not the image of fashion. It's the image of God. We are all created in the image of no less than the eternal God Himself. In Genesis, the very first book in the Bible, we read that God said, "Let us make mankind in our image, in our likeness . . . . So God created mankind in his own image. . .male and female he created them" (Genesis 1:26–27).

Being made in God's image means that our bodies are valuable, but not for what they look like. Angie Conrad writes,

I have never read any verse in scripture spelling out what constitutes a perfect body image. There are no biblical specifications of how much we should weigh, what color our hair should be, or the sizes of our noses, ears, or feet. God is concerned with the condition of our hearts, not our physical features. Although we may never fit in society's image, we are made in His image.[1]

Made in the image of God! What a privilege! Today, enjoy God's workmanship in you.

[1]Angie Conrad, "The Not-So-Perfect Image," *Tapestry Magazine* (Atlanta, GA: Vol. 13, Number 1, January 2006).

28

They speak of the glorious splendor of your majesty—
and I will meditate on your wonderful works.

PSALM 145:5

wonder—and worship!

"Oh Terri, just look at that gorgeous rose! See the delicate markings and shading? Just *look* at it!"

Terri, my walking partner, is getting used to my exclamations as we pass by lovely flowers. She knows I just *have* to exclaim about them. And she knows she might as well stop right where she is until I've had time to take a closer look.

Flowers don't catch her attention, but beautiful skies do. Several times we've taken a second loop to the top of a hill for another look at unusual cloud formations or the changing colors of the sunrise. Sometimes it seems we can peer into heaven itself.

I'm the same way about majestic mountains, multicolored tropical fish, or a new baby. Enjoying beauty takes me out of the doldrums and lifts my eyes and my heart from the muck I'm slogging through to the loveliness of God's handiwork—and ultimately to God Himself.

The created world tells us what God is like. The Bible says, "For since the creation of the world God's invisible qualities—his eternal power and divine nature—have been clearly seen, being understood from what has been made" (Romans 1:20).

King David said, "I will meditate on your wonderful works" (Psalm 145:5). Right now you can look out your window and see something God has created, even if it's only a scrap of blue sky or tiny blades of grass that have pushed their way through cracks in the concrete of a busy road.

Let the beauty you see lead you to worship the One who made it all. Go take a look.

29

*"Since you are precious and honored in my sight,
and because I love you, I will give people in exchange
for you, nations in exchange for your life."*

ISAIAH 43:4

precious

When I was growing up, a family friend had a dog she named "Precious." My dad would almost get sick whenever he heard her call the dog by that name. She was a rather homely little animal, and besides, he reasoned, "Precious" is much too sentimental, gushy, and syrupy a name for any dog.

Believe it or not, that prompted me to look up the word *precious* in my Bible concordance to see how the word is used in scripture. Not surprisingly, it is used to describe jewels and rare metals, and in many other ways as well.

In the Old Testament, when Leah's sixth son was born, she said, "God has presented me with a precious gift" (Genesis 30:20). Job said—and he knew this from experience—that a smile in the time of trouble is precious (Job 29:24). Life is also called "precious" (Psalm 22:20; 35:17), as is death, for the Bible says, "Precious in the sight of the LORD is the death of his faithful servants" (Psalm 116:15). Wisdom is more precious than rubies (Proverbs 3:15; 8:11). God's words are "more precious . . .than much pure gold" (Psalm 19:10), and so are His "very great and precious promises" (2 Peter 1:4).

It's not surprising that the blood of Christ is also called precious (1 Peter 1:19). In fact, Jesus Himself is called the "precious cornerstone" of the Church, or Body of Christ (1 Peter 2:6–7). And last, Peter speaks of our faith as being precious (2 Peter 1:1).

There's one more thing in scripture that God says is precious—you! God says, "You are precious and honored in my sight. . .and. . .I love you" (Isaiah 43:4).

Take that thought with you today!

30

He got up, rebuked the wind and said to the waves,
"Quiet! Be still!" Then the wind died down
and it was completely calm.

MARK 4:39
(THE WHOLE STORY: MARK 4:35–39)

GOD HEARS

Jesus was tired. He had taught large crowds of people gathered at the Sea of Galilee, and when evening came, He said to His disciples, "Let us go over to the other side." So they left the crowd behind and rode a boat across the lake. Jesus was so tired that He put His head on a cushion and went to sleep.

A strong squall came up and waves broke over the boat, so that it was nearly swamped. Jesus slept on. Finally the disciples woke Him. "Teacher, don't you care if we drown?" they asked. Immediately Jesus stood up, rebuked the wind, and said to the waves, "Quiet! Be still!" Then the wind died down and it was completely calm (Mark 4:35–39).

To me, the remarkable truth from this story is not merely that the storm obeyed the command of Jesus. That is, of course, amazing! But the thought that comforts me is that although the howling of the wind and the splashing of the waves didn't waken Jesus, the cries of the men in trouble did.

Like a mother who at night can tune out the din of traffic outside but waken at the slightest whimper of her baby, the Lord responds to the needs, fears, and cries of His children.

Isn't that comforting? The psalmist said, "The righteous cry out, and the LORD hears them; he delivers them from all their troubles" (Psalm 34:17). The God of heaven hears when you call. If the storm in your life is about to swamp your boat, call the One who said to the wind and waves, "Quiet! Be still."

31

*"But blessed is the one who trusts in
the LORD, whose confidence is in him."*

JEREMIAH 17:7

WHAT KIND OF CONFIDENCE?

I read a book where the author suggested that you replace negative, condemning thoughts about yourself with positive, encouraging thoughts to raise your self-esteem. She believes that by visualizing what you want your life to be, you can change it. I tried it but I have found that thinking positively about myself is not enough. Too often I cannot live up to even my own expectations.

Another author, Deborah Smith Pegues, who has been successful in the corporate world, presents a different viewpoint:

*For many years I was a staunch advocate of self-confidence. I
embraced the teachings of secular motivational speakers who
convinced me that if I believed in myself, the sky was the
limit in. . .what I could accomplish. However, having faced*

several. . .situations that required greater skills, knowledge, and mental fortitude than I possessed, I began to realize that my self-confidence was woefully inadequate.[1]

She explains that the core meaning of the word "confidence" is "with faith" and that the focus of our faith should be God, not ourselves, since God says, "Apart from me you can do nothing" (John 15:5). She adds, "The most detrimental quality we can have is self-confidence." Instead, we need to replace self-confidence with Supreme confidence—a personal confidence based on our confidence in God.

Do you have self-confidence or Supreme confidence? The Bible says, "Blessed is the one who trusts in the Lord, whose confidence is in him" (Jeremiah 17:7). His work in your life is the most positive thinking you can have.

[1]Deborah Smith Pegues, *Conquering Insecurity* (Eugene, OR: Harvest House Publishers, 2005), 122.

32

*"So if the Son sets you free,
you will be free indeed."*

JOHN 8:36

FREEDOM!

Perhaps you think of the Bible as a book full of only rules and regulations. It tells you to stop doing what you want and insists that you start doing what you have no interest in doing.

I have good news for you. Yes, there are rules in the Bible. They were put there so that we would know what God's standards are. But God knew we could never keep all His laws. So God sent His Son to earth to die on the cross to pay for our sins. He offers us forgiveness for all that we have done wrong—yes, all of it. When we ask His forgiveness and place our faith in Him, He puts the Holy Spirit in our hearts to help us obey and live for Him. That's real freedom! No more need to put up with guilty feelings. No more fear that God is out to "get you" when you mess up.

If you have placed your faith in Jesus Christ to forgive your sins, you have freedom to come to God, who loves you deeply and will forgive you when you ask Him. Even people who already have a relationship with Jesus sometimes forget that they don't have to carry around a load of guilty feelings. Keep your conscience clean by confessing any known sin to the Lord.

Don't live another day as a slave to sin and guilt. Find the true freedom that comes from knowing you are totally forgiven. Jesus, the Son of God, said, "If the Son sets you free, you will be free indeed" (John 8:36).

33

See what great love the Father has lavished on us, that we should be called children of God! And that is what we are! The reason the world does not know us is that it did not know him.

1 John 3:1

The Retirement Years?

In a book I read about the various seasons of our lives, the author referred to our sixties as the decade for preparing for retirement. I couldn't help smiling as I thought, *That author has not yet experienced being in her sixties, or she would know that for most of us who are in this period of life, they are years filled with far more than preparing for retirement.*

I'm past seventy now, and so far, retirement is not in my vocabulary. Of course, I'm realistic enough to know that eventually I'll have to slow down. But right now my husband and I still carry a full load of travel, writing, radio broadcasts, seminars, and speaking at churches and conferences. It is truly a joy for us to continue what we so enjoy doing.

But what if we were hit with an injury or disabling disease that changed all this? What if we had to limit our outreach and stay home because we were not physically able to continue? Would we be less valuable to God? No, not at all. All of us are valuable to God because He loves us for who we are—His children, made in His image—not for what we accomplish.

The apostle John wrote, "See what great love the Father has lavished on us, that we should be called children of God!" (1 John 3:1). No matter what your age, no matter what you can do or are unable to do, if you are God's child, He loves you in a lavish way. What more could any of us ask?

34

All have turned away, all have become corrupt;
there is no one who does good, not even one.

PSALM 14:3

THE GREAT EXCHANGE

She sat across the table from my husband and me and, with tears in her eyes, said, "I'd like to have Jesus in my heart, but I don't think I can be good enough."

"I'm so glad you told us how you feel," we told her, "because there's good news. You don't have to be good enough. None of us can be. The Bible says, 'There is no one who does good, not even one' (Psalm 14:3). That's exactly why Jesus came to this earth—to die for our sins. He did for us what we could not do for ourselves."

Yes, Jesus came to carry on an exchange, to say to us, as only a good God can say: "You give Me your humanity and I will give you My divinity. You give Me your time and I will give you My eternity. You give Me your sin and I will give you My purity. You give Me your broken heart and I will give you My love. You give Me your nothingness and I will give you My all."

What an exchange! We give Him our brokenness, and He gives us His wholeness.

If we had to be good enough to deserve forgiveness and salvation, not one of us would qualify—not the kindest, most generous person in the world. But that's the beauty of God's exchange offer. We ask Him to take our sin, and in the greatest trade-in program in the world, He gives us His righteousness.

If you have not made that great exchange, you can do it right now. If you already have, pour out your gratitude to the Lord.

35

God made him who had no sin to be sin for us,
so that in him we might become the righteousness of God.

2 Corinthians 5:21

when god could not look

For years, Dr. Margaret Brand served as a missionary eye surgeon in southern India. In the rural areas she would sometimes do a hundred cataract surgeries in a day.

In one instance where there was no electricity, a twelve-year-old boy was asked to hold a large flashlight so that its beam gave Dr. Brand enough light to operate. Dr. Brand doubted whether the boy would be able to endure the sight of eyes being sliced open and stitched. For the first five operations he did his job impressively. During the sixth, however, he faltered.

"Little brother, show the light properly," Dr. Brand instructed him. But she could see that he simply could not bear to look at the eye. When she asked him if he was feeling well, she saw that tears were running down his cheeks. "Oh, doctor, I cannot look," replied the lad. "This one, she is my mother."[1]

When Jesus was hanging on the cross, God the Father could not look. Jesus cried out, "My God, my God, why have you forsaken me?" (Matthew 27:46). A great shadow had come between Jesus and the Father. Jesus was lonely on that cross because of you and me.

God had to turn His eyes away from His Son in those moments because of our sin. You see, "God made him who had no sin to be sin for us, so that in him we might become the righteousness of God" (2 Corinthians 5:21) through putting our faith in Him.

Have you thanked Him recently that He was willing to pay that price?

[1] Dr. Margaret E. Brand with Dr. James L. Jost, *Vision for God* (Grand Rapids, MI: Discovery House Publishers, 2006), 121.

36

*"If you, then, though you are evil, know how to give good gifts
to your children, how much more will your Father in
heaven give good gifts to those who ask him!"*

MATTHEW 7:11

TWO IMPORTANT WORDS

Kay Warren, wife of pastor and author Rick Warren, says, "In parenting, if you don't insist on anything else, insist that your kids learn to obey two words: 'Come' and 'No.'"

She explains that if your children learn to come to you when you call them and to accept your "No" when you have to deny them something they want, they will learn to obey God when He uses those same words.

How do you respond to God when you hear Him say "Come" and "No"? God calls us, saying, "Come to me, all you who are weary and burdened, and I will give you rest" (Matthew 11:28). But even though we're bone-tired from carrying a heavy load, we tell ourselves that we have no time to come to the Lord. We're much too busy. So we stubbornly muddle through in our own strength. God says, "Come," and we say, "No."

Other times it's God who says "No" to us. "Don't do that. It's not good for you." But we interpret that to mean, "God just doesn't want me to have what I want." Or we consider it "unanswered prayer," thinking God didn't hear or doesn't care.

Jesus said, "If you, then, though you are evil, know how to give good gifts to your children, how much more will your Father in heaven give good gifts to those who ask him!" (Matthew 7:11). If we want the best for our own children, surely we can understand that God wants the best for us as well.

Teach your kids to obey those two key words, "Come" and "No." As adults, let's also learn to obey those same words ourselves when we hear them from our heavenly Father.

37

LORD, our Lord, how majestic is your name in all the earth!
You have set your glory in the heavens.

PSALM 8:1

(THE WHOLE STORY: PSALM 8:1, 3–4)

HOW BIG?

Not long ago scientists discovered the largest ball of hot gas in space that has yet been found. "The size and velocity are truly fantastic,"[1] says one of the physicists.

If you were traveling at the speed of light, to cross this big ball of gas would take you—three million years! If you want to look at it another way, it's five billion times larger than our solar system. Astounding!

As you know from reading this book, I get excited when I learn about the enormity of creation because I get a hint of how great our God is. Obviously, the person who makes something is greater than what he makes, so God is greater by far than the incredible size of this newly discovered object in space.

The heavens are the work of God's fingers. We can almost picture God deciding one day to do some arts and crafts, so He created the universe.

No wonder David cried out,

> O LORD, our Lord,
> how majestic is your name in all the earth!
> You have set your glory
> in the heavens. . . .
> When I consider your heavens,
> the work of your fingers,
> the moon and the stars,
> which you have set in place,
> what is mankind that you are mindful of them,
> human beings that you care for them?
> PSALM 8:1, 3–4

God does care. I don't know how big a problem you're dealing with today. But I can assure you of one thing: God is bigger—and He cares. Talk to Him about it now.

[1]John Johnson, Jr., "Great Ball of Fire: X-Rays Spot Mass of Gas 5 Billion Times Larger Than Solar System," *Los Angeles Times*, June 17, 2006, A15.

38

*[The Lord] satisfies your desires with good things
so that your youth is renewed like the eagle's.*

PSALM 103:5

THINGS WE LIKE TO EAT

Before we began eating our meals together, my dad bowed his head. I can still hear his deep voice as he prayed,

*For things we like to eat,
Thy loving gift of food,
We thank Thee, Lord, today,
For Thou art kind and good.
Amen.[1]*

He was eighty-eight years old and still praying a prayer that he taught me when I was a little girl. We used to say it out loud together as a family. Recently, I came across the book from which that prayer was taken, and the memory came back.

Although I no longer pray those exact words, I realize how many times I still thank the Lord for food that I really like to eat. My husband and I travel a lot, and when we do, we eat some. . .well, let's say "unusual" foods. Most of them are good but some are pretty strange to our taste. When I come back home after times like that, the prayer springs from my heart, "Thank You, Lord, for food that I *like* to eat. It tastes so good!"

Maybe you eat gourmet cuisine prepared by an outstanding chef. Maybe your food is simple fare—bread or rice and a bit of meat and vegetables. Regardless of how expensive or cheap our food may be, you'd probably agree that the best-tasting meals are those we really like. But let us not forget that our food is a gift from the Lord because He loves and cares for us.

The psalmist said God "satisfies your desires with good things so that your youth is renewed like the eagle's" (Psalm 103:5). Thank You, Lord, for good-tasting food!

[1]Mary Alice Jones, ed., *Prayers for Little Children* (Chicago, IL: Rand McNally Company, 1937), 59.

39

But God demonstrates his own love for us in this:
While we were still sinners, Christ died for us.

ROMANS 5:8

WHY DOESN'T GOD TELL US?

Many of the "whys" of life are totally beyond our comprehension: a toddler run over by a car, a jetliner crashing because birds flew into its engines, violent earthquakes. Animals don't ask, "Why?" They just endure. But God gave human beings the ability to ask, "Why?" Our difficulty is that we have a mind that asks questions, but we do not have enough insight to understand the answers.

I believe that God set life up this way as a test of faith. If we could understand the answers to all our "whys," we would not have to trust Him. Someday we'll understand because then we'll have the perspective of eternity. In the meantime, trusting God with the "whys" is the ultimate test of whether or not we believe He is trustworthy.

So, what do you do with all your "whys"? Ruth Bell Graham, wife of evangelist Billy Graham, put it so beautifully when she wrote,

I lay my "whys?"
before Your cross
in worship kneeling,
my mind beyond all hope,
my heart beyond all feeling;
and worshipping,
realize that I,
in knowing You,
don't need a "why?"[1]

The cross is the ultimate "why?"—Why would God send His Son to die for us? Romans 5:8 says, "But God demonstrates his own love for us in this: While we were still sinners, Christ died for us." God's love for us gives us the confidence that He has our ultimate good at heart.

[1]Ruth Bell Graham, *Collected Poems* (Grand Rapids, MI: Baker Books, 1997), 262.

40

Blessed is the one whose transgressions
are forgiven, whose sins are covered.

PSALM 32:1
(THE WHOLE STORY: PSALM 32:1–5)

MISERY—AND RELIEF!

Remember when you were a kid and you'd done something wrong? You knew when you got home you'd have to face your parents—and the consequences—so you took the longest route home, dragging your feet all the way. You were miserable.

Well, that doesn't happen only when you're a kid. When we've done something that we know displeases God, we're also miserable—until we come near to Him and settle it with Him.

King David experienced all of that. He knew he had done wrong, and for days he avoided dealing with it. He describes his misery in these poetic words: "When I kept silent, my bones wasted away through my groaning all day long. For day and night your hand was heavy upon me; my strength was sapped as in the heat of summer" (Psalm 32:3–4). Oh yes, David, that's what a guilty conscience feels like!

But David decided to deal with his wrongdoing. He tells us, "Then I acknowledged my sin to you and did not cover up my iniquity. I said, 'I will confess my transgressions to the LORD.' And you forgave the guilt of my sin" (verse 5). Relief at last!

Maybe right now you are as miserable as David was. You're not on speaking terms with God because there's an issue you and He need to settle—a barrier between you and Him. What are you waiting for? Quit dragging your feet. Right now, come home to the Father, confess your sin, and find His forgiveness and restoration, His comfort and closeness. Then, with David, you can say, "Blessed is the one whose transgressions are forgiven, whose sins are covered" (Psalm 32:1).

41

What other nation is so great as to have
their gods near them the way the LORD our
God is near us whenever we pray to him?

DEUTERONOMY 4:7

WHERE IS GOD WHEN WE PRAY?

When we pray, sometimes we strongly sense God's presence right with us. Other times God seems very far away. Somebody quipped, "If God seems far away, guess who moved!" But I don't think that is true. That's like saying, if you can't "feel" God's presence, then He must not be there. Feelings follow faith; they don't precede it.

The prophet Moses declared that God is *always* near us when we pray: "What other nation is so great as to have their gods near them the way the LORD our God is near us whenever we pray to him?" (Deuteronomy 4:7).

The vastness of space can make you feel that God must be beyond our universe—He must be a great distance from where you are when you pray. Don't believe this feeling for a moment. Our God is big enough to be everywhere at the same time.

When King David tried to think of a place where God is not, he gave up, saying,

> *Where can I go from your Spirit?*
> *Where can I flee from your presence?*
> *If I go up to the heavens, you are there;*
> *if I make my bed in the depths, you are there.*
> *If I rise on the wings of the dawn,*
> *if I settle on the far side of the sea,*
> *even there your hand will guide me,*
> *your right hand will hold me fast.*
>
> PSALM 139:7–10

So, when you pray, don't base whether or not God is listening on your feelings. As Moses said, "the LORD our God is near us whenever we pray to him," listening to every word.

42

On the first day of every week, each one of you
should set aside a sum of money in keeping
with your income, saving it up, so that when
I come no collections will have to be made.

1 Corinthians 16:2

HOW MUCH SHOULD YOU GIVE?

How much of your money should you give away? That's a question worth thinking over because the Bible gives clear instructions on giving: "Each of you should give what you have decided in your heart to give, not reluctantly or under compulsion, for God loves a cheerful giver" (2 Corinthians 9:7).

Growing up as a preacher's kid, I sometimes sat by myself in church, with my dad leading the service and my mom playing the organ. One Sunday, one of the choir members left her purse on the seat next to mine so she could sit with me during the sermon. When offering time came, however, she was still seated in the choir loft watching helplessly as, unprompted, I opened her purse and took out money for the offering—I have no memory of how much. She gave, but I don't know how cheerfully.

In the Old Testament giving was to be a tithe—that is, 10 percent of your income for the Lord. But in the New Testament Paul wrote, "On the first day of every week, each one of you should set aside a sum of money *in keeping with your income*" (1 Corinthians 16:2, italics added).

Actually, tithing isn't totally fair. If a person makes five hundred dollars a month and gives fifty dollars of it, it is a sacrifice. But if a rich man makes fifty thousand dollars a month and gives five thousand dollars of it, he still has forty-five thousand dollars left to spend. That's why the Bible says our giving should be in keeping with our income.

The famous Bible teacher G. Campbell Morgan wrote, "Test all your giving by your own prosperity."[1] It's a good rule for deciding how much money you should give.

---

[1]G. Campbell Morgan, *The Corinthian Letters of Paul* (New York: Fleming H. Revell Company, 1946), 209.

43

How beautiful on the mountains are the feet of those who bring good news, who proclaim peace, who bring good tidings, who proclaim salvation, who say to Zion, "Your God reigns!"

ISAIAH 52:7

A BEAUTIFUL WOMAN

Evelyn Harris was a well-off, beautiful woman. So beautiful was she that artists competed for the privilege of painting her portrait.

But with her husband, Jesse Brand, she left the luxuries of London to become a missionary among the hill people of India. There, she bore Paul, who at age nine went to England for schooling. During this time, Jesse died from fever, and Evelyn returned to London—a woman beaten by pain and grief. When Paul saw her again, he thought, *Could this bent, haggard woman possibly be my mother?*

Against all advice, Evelyn went back to India, nursing the sick, rearing orphans, pulling teeth, clearing jungle land, and preaching the gospel. She traveled constantly, sleeping under a tiny mosquito net shelter. By this time Paul had become a gifted doctor to the lepers of India. When his mother broke her hip at age seventy-five, Paul asked her, "Shouldn't you think about retiring?" But no argument could dissuade her.

"Paul, if I leave, who will help the village people? In any case, why preserve this old body if it's not going to be used where God needs me?" It was her final answer.

Paul wrote of her, "In old age Mother was thin and crippled, her face furrowed with deep wrinkles. And yet I can truly say that Evelyn Harris Brand was a beautiful woman, to the very end."

At ninety-five Evelyn died and was buried among her people.[1] As the Bible says, "How beautiful on the mountains are the feet of those. . .who proclaim salvation" (Isaiah 52:7).

[1]Dr. Paul Brand and Philip Yancey, *The Gift of Pain* (Manila, Philippines: OMF Literature Inc., 2000), 306–9.

44

The man of God replied, "The LORD
can give you much more than that."

2 CHRONICLES 25:9

GOD IS ABLE TO GIVE
YOU MUCH MORE

Amaziah, the king of Judah, was headed to war with three
hundred thousand soldiers. But he didn't think this was enough,
so he hired another one hundred thousand from the nation of
Israel, for which he paid a tidy sum that amounted to between
three and four tons of silver.

About this time a man of God came along, and when he
found out that Amaziah had hired troops from Israel, he told
the king that God was not in this—that if he let the Israelite
soldiers fight with their troops, they would be defeated.

"But," asked Amaziah, "what about the hundred talents I paid for these Israelite troops?" The man of God replied, "The LORD can give you much more than that" (2 Chronicles 25:9).

Amaziah hated to lose his money but he obeyed the man of God and sent the Israelite troops home, and God gave him a great victory.

Aren't we all tempted at times to take shortcuts with God? Maybe you're tempted not to give money to missions because there is something else for which you think you need to spend the money. Remember, the Lord can give you much more than that. Maybe, like me, you're tempted to cut your prayer time short because there's something else you think you need to get done. You and I should remember that if we put Him first, God is able to give us much more efficiency in our day so that we accomplish much more.

We must simply do the right thing, trusting God at any cost for all the rest—because God is able to give us much more in return.

45

*"You may ask me for anything
in my name, and I will do it."*

John 14:14

GOD KEEPS HIS WORD

Heather Reynolds, of a ministry called God's Golden Acre, has helped countless of orphaned Zulu children in South Africa. Here's a story about her that will inspire you.

God's Golden Acre desperately needed sand to complete the refurbishing of one of the center's buildings. A volunteer, who was an atheist, challenged Heather, "Why don't you ask your God to provide the sand if you have no money to buy some?"

Heather said to herself, *This young man is quite right. God, why don't You answer our prayers? Do You want me to beg?* She picked up the phone and called the local building supply—for the third time—asking for a load of sand as a donation. She was told "No" and adamantly told not to call again.

About half an hour later Heather was disturbed by loud laughter outside on the grounds.

"What's all this about?" asked Heather, going outside.

"It's your miracle," said the atheist volunteer. "You see that man walking through the gate over there? He's the driver of a ten-ton truck of sand, and his truck has just broken down on our driveway. He has asked our permission to tip all this sand so his company can tow the truck away." Ironically, it was the same company from which Heather had just asked for sand.[1]

One of Heather's favorite Bible promises is John 14:14: "You may ask me for anything in my name, and I will do it." Heather has proved that God keeps His word!

[1]Dale le Vack, *God's Golden Acre* (Oxford, UK, and Grand Rapids, MI: Monarch Books, 2005), 244–45.

46

*Those the LORD has rescued will return. They will enter
Zion with singing; everlasting joy will crown their
heads. Gladness and joy will overtake them,
and sorrow and sighing will flee away.*

ISAIAH 35:10

OBSOLETE!

Was last night sleepless for you because you've recently lost
someone dear to you? Weeks may have even passed since
you said goodbye, but you've not been able to process the
grief. You spend most nights crying, and even now, the tears
are flowing.

If it seems to you that you will never get over your grief,
I want to remind you there's a day coming when "sorrow and
sighing will flee away" (Isaiah 35:10). Did that thought really
sink into your heart—that one day the words *sorrow* and *sighing*
will be forever gone from our vocabulary?

Famous London preacher Joseph Parker said that when you look through a dictionary, you will sometimes come across a word that is marked "obsolete." That means the word is outdated and no one uses it anymore. There will come a day, Parker said, when *sorrow* and *sighing* will be two words we will never use again.[1] Revelation 21:4 gives us four more words: " 'There will be no more *death* or *mourning* or *crying* or *pain*.' " (italics added). All obsolete! Archaic! Forgotten!

In the meantime, know that the Lord is near you during this difficult time. He knows how you feel. When He was in the Garden of Gethsemane before He was crucified, the Bible says that He "offered up prayers and petitions with fervent cries and tears" (Hebrews 5:7). He understands. The Bible tells us, "The Lord is close to the brokenhearted and saves those who are crushed in spirit" (Psalm 34:18).

Come to Him. Let Him hold you close to His heart.

[1] R. W. De Haan, *Our Daily Bread* (Grand Rapids, MI: Radio Bible Class, September 11, 1969).

47

"Remember these things, Jacob, for you, Israel, are my servant.
I have made you, you are my servant; Israel,
I will not forget you."

ISAIAH 44:21

FORGOTTEN? NOT BY GOD!

When the Romans banished the apostle John to the isle of
Patmos, they must have thought he would soon be forgotten and
his influence wiped out forever. Pastor Jack Hayford points out,

> *A small mountainous island with rocky soil in the Aegean*
> *Sea, Patmos should have remained an anonymous piece*
> *of land that people were sent to and never heard from again.*
> *. . . But God had other ideas.*[1]

In this most unlikely location, John wrote the last book
of the New Testament, Revelation, which tells what must take
place in the end times.

Today John would be astounded to see that Patmos is a vacation spot, where tourists flock to see the place where God revealed Himself to him in such an outstanding way.

If you're in a difficult-to-understand situation right now, take hope. Like John, you may feel you've been taken out of the mainstream of life—sidelined. Perhaps your life is consumed in caring for a loved one so severely disabled that he or she doesn't recognize who you are. Or maybe you've had to discontinue teaching a Bible study that was the joy of your life. Or maybe you feel exiled to a job you hate but can't quit because you need the money.

To His people God says, "I have made you. . . I will not forget you" (Isaiah 44:21).

Feel forgotten? Not by God! Wherever is your "Patmos," remember that while you are there God has you clearly in His sight. Someday He will bring blessing from your banishment.

[1]Jack Hayford, from an address at the twentieth anniversary commencement of Angelus Bible Institute, Los Angeles, CA, 2006.

48

To proclaim the year of the LORD's favor. . .
to comfort all who mourn, and. . .to bestow on
them a crown of beauty instead of ashes, the oil
of joy instead of mourning, and a garment
of praise instead of a spirit of despair.

ISAIAH 61:2–3

Unnecessarily Beautiful

Missionary doctor Margaret Brand writes of the time when her young son, Christopher, was outside playing in the hill country of India toward sunset time: "He rushed in excitedly. . . and tried to drag me outside as he almost shouted, 'Come see the sky. It's unnecessarily beautiful!'. . . His words have stayed with me ever since."[1]

God created beauty beyond anything the human mind could have imagined—truly unnecessarily beautiful. Some of the loveliest places on earth are so remote that they have never been seen by anyone, yet God still made them beautiful.

But you don't have to go far to see beauty. Think of where you live. What beauty has God brought into your life? Something as simple as a rose? Spectacular lightning? A beautiful view of the ocean? Perhaps God's unnecessary beauty in your life is as basic as having food that you *like*, not just food that keeps you alive. I mean, did you ever thank God for chocolate?

The Old Testament prophet Isaiah foretold some seven hundred years before Jesus was born that He would be appointed "to comfort all who mourn. . .to bestow on them a crown of beauty instead of ashes, the oil of joy instead of mourning, and a garment of praise instead of a spirit of despair" (Isaiah 61:2–3).

These comforting words tell of the Lord's blessings far beyond anything we deserve. Take a moment to thank Him for some specific beauty that He has blessed you with—unnecessary, perhaps—above and beyond anything you expected.

[1]Dr. Margaret E. Brand with Dr. James L. Jost, *Vision for God* (Grand Rapids, MI: Discovery House Publishers, 2006), 108.

49

"Greater love has no one than this:
to lay down one's life for one's friends."

JOHN 15:13

NO GREATER LOVE

Robert McQuilken was serving as president of Columbia Bible College when his wife, Muriel, developed Alzheimer's disease. Becoming increasingly confused, at last she could form only one sentence. But she said it often: "I love you."

After Robert would leave for work, Muriel would often walk to where he was—a one-mile round trip that she would sometimes make ten times a day. At night, he would see that her feet were bruised and bloodied. Finally he decided that he could no longer keep his position and care for Muriel at the same time, so he resigned from the college, saying, "Had I not promised, forty-two years before, 'in sickness and in health... till death do us part'?"[1]

McQuilken was criticized. Other people could take care of Muriel, his critics said, but not everyone could fill his shoes at the school. Soon she would not even know who he was, so why should he give up his ministry in order to care for her?

He answered them,

> *It's not that I have to, it's that I get to. I love her very dearly. . . . It's a great honor to care for such a wonderful person.*[2] *Muriel is the joy of my life.*[3]

Robert McQuilken's love and sacrifice for his wife draw us to reflect on Jesus' love for us. Jesus said, "Greater love has no one than this: to lay down one's life for one's friends" (John 15:13). That is exactly what He did for us. We're not always very lovable. In fact, sometimes we're downright difficult. Yet He loves us—not because He *has* to but because He *wants* to.

[1]John Tucker, Pastor, October 3, 2004, Milford Baptist Church, North Shore Auckland, NZ http://www.milfordbaptist.co.nz/sermon_20041003.htm, accessed July 16, 2008.
[2]http://www.youtube.com/watch?v=f6pX1phIqug, accessed October 9, 2008
[3]John Tucker, ibid.

50

He will swallow up death forever. The Sovereign LORD will wipe away the tears from all faces; he will remove his people's disgrace from all the earth. The LORD has spoken.

ISAIAH 25:8

no more tears

Joey O'Connor was exhausted. He had just come home from the memorial service for a close friend who had been killed in a freak boating accident. Worn out by grief, Joey flopped down on the bed to spend a few quiet moments with his three-year-old daughter, Janae. Immediately she began to ask questions about the accident and Joel's death.

"Where's heaven?"

"Well, I don't know exactly where heaven is," Joey admitted, "but I can tell you what heaven is like." Then he explained that the Bible promises heaven to be a place where we will live with God forever. That there's no death in heaven, no pain or ow-ees or scraped knees, and finally, that there are no tears because it is a wonderful, happy place with nothing to make us sad.

Suddenly the light came on for Janae. "Yeah," she responded, "heaven's *not* a crying place."[1]

You have it right, Janae. The prophet Isaiah tells us that in the life to come God "will swallow up death forever. The sovereign LORD will wipe away the tears from all faces."

And then like a signature to his statement, he adds, "The LORD has spoken" (Isaiah 25:8).

The book of Revelation tells us that God "'will wipe every tear from their eyes. There will be no more death' or mourning or crying or pain, for the old order of things has passed away" (Revelation 21:4).

On earth, tears are a God-given outlet for the pain that we experience, but heaven's "not a crying place." It's God's promise.

[1]Joey O'Connor, *Heaven's Not a Crying Place* (Grand Rapids, MI: Fleming H. Revell, 1997), 15–19.

51

*My times are in your hands; deliver me from the hands
of my enemies, from those who pursue me.*

PSALM 31:15

IN THE NICK OF TIME

She was desperate. Deciding that life wasn't worth living any longer, she climbed up to where she could loop a pair of pantyhose over the rafters. Now she was ready to tie them around her neck and jump.

But her radio was on, and the speaker's words caught her attention. The message was only five minutes—*Guidelines*, a radio program that my husband has been producing for more than fifty years. The topic that day was—"What God Thinks of Suicide."

Instead of jumping, the woman called the radio station. The technician airing the program that day answered the call and in the next few moments led her to faith in Christ. Since that time she has visited the station, and it's been confirmed—she is a changed person!

Think of the timing of that incident. The program had been written several months earlier in order to meet programming deadlines. After the recording session, a *Guidelines* volunteer listened to be sure there were no grammatical errors or technical blips. Then a CD had to be produced and mailed to the station. Of course, there's the fact that the technician chose to air that program on that day. And the program went on the air at exactly the time the woman was about to end her life. No accident!

God makes no mistakes, for He is a God of precision. The psalmist wrote, "My times are in your hands" (Psalm 31:15). He can manage the timing in your life. Put your life in His hands and trust Him.

52

Be kind and compassionate to one another, forgiving each other, just as in Christ God forgave you.

EPHESIANS 4:32

FREEDOM OF FORGIVENESS

Author Ray Pritchard tells about an old monk and his young apprentice who were walking together along a trail. When they came to a river with a fast current, they saw an old woman weeping near the shoreline because she could not cross the river on her own. Their monastery had a rule forbidding all contact with women. Nevertheless, the older monk picked her up and, without a word, carried her to the other side.

The old woman went on her way, and the monk and his apprentice proceeded on their journey. Neither said a word but on the inside, the young monk was seething. When he could stand it no longer, he blurted out, "My lord, why did you carry that woman across the river? You know that we are not supposed to touch a woman." The wise old monk looked down at the young man and said, "I put her down hours ago. Why are you still carrying her?"[1]

Like the young monk, you too may be carrying a burden from your past. Someone wounded you deeply; they were wrong and you were right, yet you are still carrying the load of your unforgiveness. Alan Paton said, "When a deep injury is done to us, we never recover until we forgive."[2] Physical, emotional, and even spiritual problems will continue to plague us until we forgive. Even though the person who wronged us has done nothing to deserve our forgiveness, the Bible says we should "be kind and compassionate to one another, forgiving each other, just as in Christ God forgave you" (Ephesians 4:32).

If Jesus could hang on the cross and pray, "Father, forgive them," can we do less?

[1]Ray Pratchard, *The Healing Power of Forgiveness* (Eugene, OR: Harvest House Publishers, 2005), 138.
[2]Ibid., 129.

53

"Be perfect, therefore, as your
heavenly Father is perfect."

MATTHEW 5:48

STOLEN IDENTITY

I hope you have never opened your mail and had to say, "I certainly didn't buy those items with my credit card!" If that happened to you, you were the victim of stolen identity. Someone used your name and personal information to commit fraud.

Identity theft can happen anywhere to anyone. If it occurs, you spend hundreds of hours cleaning up your credit and getting back your good name.

But what about your personal identity—not just what you own but who you are? That's the most important identity of all. Author Kendry Smiley asks,

Where is your identity? Is it in your purse or in your family or in your speaking or writing? Is it in your achievements or awards or titles or accolades? If it is, someone can steal it! If your identity is in the Lord, it can never be stolen.[1]

No matter how successful you may be, remember that your achievements—whether measured by how wonderful your children turned out, or how successful your career is, or how much cash and jewelry you own—have been possible only by God's grace. God is the One who has given you the talent, the intelligence, the health, and the opportunities to be who you are.

Jesus said, "Be perfect, therefore, as your heavenly Father is perfect" (Matthew 5:48). The word *perfect* means "complete." I like the way *The Message* translation of the verse puts it: "Live out your God-created identity. Live generously and graciously toward others, the way God lives toward you." God-created identity can never be stolen.

Be who you are with your whole heart—for God's glory.

---

[1]Kendry Smiley, quoted in *The Woman Behind the Mask* by Jan Coleman (Grand Rapids, MI: Kregel Publications, 2005), 105.

54

"Do not worship any other god, for the LORD,
whose name is Jealous, is a jealous God."

EXODUS 34:14

WHEN JEALOUSY ISN'T SIN

We usually think of jealousy as a bad thing—a sin. On the contrary, you may be surprised to know that the Bible says God Himself is jealous. But He's jealous for the right reasons. You see, God loves deeply, and when you love someone intensely, you are jealous of anything or anyone who would steal from you the one you love.

God warned Moses, "Do not worship any other god, for the LORD, whose name is Jealous, is a jealous God" (Exodus 34:14). If I love anything—any person, any activity, any idea more than I love God, He sees this as infidelity or unfaithfulness. God says, "I have been grieved by their adulterous hearts" (Ezekiel 6:9)—hearts that prefer something or someone else to Him.

Bible teacher G. Campbell Morgan says jealousy is a word that is similar to the word "zealous."[1] Another synonym is "passionate"—the opposite of being apathetic or indifferent. In the vernacular we say God is "crazy about us."

Jealousy can be a good thing. I'm glad to know my husband is jealous of my love—that is, he doesn't want to share my love with anyone else. God is that way too. His heart is pleased when our love for Him is fervent, real, and passionate! Not love that evaporates when difficulty heats up or the events of the day take precedence.

It's hard to admit that sometimes we do prefer someone or something else to God. Maybe if we reflect on that as infidelity, we'll think twice before choosing something instead of our God. Think about it.

[1] G. Campbell Morgan, *The Corinthian Letters of Paul* (New York: Fleming H. Revell Company, 1946), 130.

55

Praise be to the God and Father of our Lord Jesus Christ,
the Father of compassion and the God of all comfort.

2 CORINTHIANS 1:3

THE COMFORTER

After our grandson Christian was born, I gave his mother, Cheryl, a soft and cozy robe to wear when she got up at night to care for him.

Within a few months, however, Christian had decided that her new robe was what he would like to hold when he needed comfort. The robe was floor-length, so Cheryl simply cut twelve inches or so off the bottom for Christian to enjoy, still leaving her a robe to wear—or so she thought. The problem was that while Christian was okay with having "little robe" with him in the car, he wanted "big robe" when he went to sleep at night. Being the grandma, my solution was to buy Cheryl another robe.

As adults, we'd get some strange looks if we carried around a robe with us for comfort. But what—or who—can we hold on to when we need comforting? No less than God Himself—"the Father of compassion and the God of all comfort" (2 Corinthians 1:3). He welcomes us when circumstances are more than we can handle. All we have to do is put aside our high and mighty independence, come to God, and ask Him for His help. The beloved hymn "What a Friend We Have in Jesus" says,

> O what peace we often forfeit,
> O what needless pain we bear,
> All because we do not carry
> Everything to God in prayer![1]

Don't be ashamed to call on God for comfort when your heart is aching. He waits for you with open arms. Run to Him and let Him hold you close to His heart.

---

[1]Joseph M. Scriven, *The Hymnal for Worship & Celebration* (Waco, TX: Word Music, 1986), 435.

56

Those who know your name trust in you, for you, LORD,
have never forsaken those who seek you.

PSALM 9:10

Never Forsaken

Chris Haggai was feeding Johnny, her adult son who had
cerebral palsy, when a visitor arrived. The woman had come to
take a look at a refrigerator the Haggais had just purchased
because she was thinking of buying one like it. Chris had to
continue feeding Johnny but told the visitor she could look at
the refrigerator. The woman, however, became curious about
Johnny.

"How do you ever cope?" the visitor asked.

"With Johnny? He's a darling!" Chris gave Johnny a loving
pinch on the cheek. Just then Johnny choked up some of his
food—something that happened at least once a day. Chris
hurried to make him comfortable.

"He must take hours of your day," the visitor said.

"God permits things for a purpose in our lives," Chris told her. "If I'm faithful, God will bless me for that faithfulness. If I refuse to accept what God permits, I'll be the loser."

After a few moments, Chris turned and found her visitor at the point of tears. "My husband died six months ago of a heart attack," the woman said. "I've been blaming God for taking my husband away from me."[1]

Chris shared deeply from her experiences and from the Bible about acceptance and trusting God. Before the visitor left, she had committed her life to Christ and began to understand that she could trust God to bring good from even the most painful experiences of life.

The psalmist wrote, "Those who know your name trust in you, for you, LORD, have never forsaken those who seek you" (Psalm 9:10). Wonderful assurance!

[1]John Edmund Haggai, *My Son Johnny* (Wheaton, IL: Tyndale House Publishers, Inc. 1978), 109–11.

57

This is what the LORD says. . . "If only you had paid attention to
my commands, your peace would have been like a river,
your well-being like the waves of the sea."

ISAIAH 48:17–18

IF ONLY . . .

A young woman in her twenties told me that she really has no choice but to obey God because when she doesn't, she is the loser. At a young age she has figured out the very important principle that God's will, as difficult as it may sometimes be, is always the best for us.

God longs to bring good into our lives. In Isaiah we read,

This is what the LORD says—
your Redeemer, the Holy One of Israel:
"I am the LORD your God,

> *who teaches you what is best for you,*
> *who directs you in the way you should go.*
> *If only you had paid attention to my commands,*
> *your peace would have been like a river,*
> *your well-being like the waves of the sea."*
> ISAIAH 48:17–18

"If only..." God says. If only you had not married that guy who doesn't share your faith.... If only you had pursued God's will for your life when you still had the chance to choose the direction your life would go.... If only you had shown more patience and tenderness toward your kids while they were still living at home...

Well, we can't go back and unscramble scrambled eggs. What's done is done. But you can make a decision that from this point on, with His help, you will obey God and choose to do His will.

Remember that He is the Lord your God, who "teaches you what is best for you, who directs you in the way you should go." Look to Him for guidance. Obey Him and find peace.

58

For since the beginning of the world men have not heard nor perceived by the ear, nor has the eye seen any God besides You, who acts for the one who waits for Him.

ISAIAH 64:4 NKJV

THE GOD WHO ACTS ON OUR BEHALF

Some people say, "All roads lead to God, so it doesn't matter which religion you follow as long as you're seeking God." But a wise prophet in Old Testament times strongly disagreed. He declared that the God of the Bible is different from all other gods. Isaiah said: "For since the beginning of the world men have not heard nor perceived by the ear, nor has the eye seen any God besides You, who acts for the one who waits for Him" (Isaiah 64:4 NKJV).

Isaiah asserted that other gods don't do anything to help their followers. They don't answer their prayers. On the contrary, these gods *demand* much from their followers, requiring sacrificial offerings, good works in order to achieve higher ranking, and sometimes even their very lives. But the one true God as revealed in the Bible cares about those who put their trust in Him and acts on their behalf.

Our God has power over everything in the universe, over the gods people worship—and over your problems as well. I like the perspective of the person who said, "Don't tell God how big your troubles are—tell your troubles *how big your God is.*"

Yes, if your God is the God of the Bible, you can count on Him to help. Just be patient a little longer. Keep waiting on God for His answer to your dilemma. Make these words your guide: "But as for me, I watch in hope for the Lord, I wait for God my Savior; my God will hear me" (Micah 7:7). The God of the universe, the God of the Bible, will answer your prayers if you expectantly and patiently wait for Him.

59

Godly men buried Stephen and mourned deeply for him.

ACTS 8:2

IS IT UNSPIRITUAL TO GRIEVE?

❦

"Is it wrong for a Christian to grieve?" author Daisy Catchings asks. "Or is faith supposed to eradicate tears?"[1]

Well, in the Bible, even men of faith grieved. Abraham wept when Sarah died. David shed many tears when his son Absalom was buried. Even Jesus wept when Lazarus was in the tomb.

To me the most remarkable incidence of grieving in the Bible occurred among believers when Stephen was stoned to death for preaching the gospel. Since Jesus' resurrection had taken place just weeks before, the truth that all believers will be resurrected was fresh in the minds of the early Christians. Stephen had even seen a vision of Jesus just before his death. Yet we read that "godly men buried Stephen and mourned deeply for him" (Acts 8:2). Knowing they would one day be reunited with Stephen didn't wipe out the reality that they were heartbroken because he was no longer with them.

The apostle Paul told the early church that he did not want them to "grieve like the rest of mankind, who have no hope" (1 Thessalonians 4:13). He didn't say, "Don't grieve"; he said not to grieve the same way people grieve who have no hope of ever seeing their loved ones again.

Psychologists will tell you that the person who suffers a great loss but does not grieve faces the dangers of mental and emotional problems. Pent-up emotions will take their toll in one way or another.

Thank the Lord that He who gave us laughter to express happiness also gave us tears as an outlet for our grief until the day when He will wipe all tears from our eyes.

[1]Daisy Catchings, *Under God's Umbrella* (Palm Springs, CA: Umbrella Ministries, 1999), 105.

60

Do not take revenge, my dear friends, but leave room
for God's wrath, for it is written: "It is mine to
avenge; I will repay," says the Lord.

ROMANS 12:19

LEAVE ROOM FOR GOD

In Robert Morgan's small but very practical book called *The Red Sea Rules* he tells about a time when he was exceptionally worried about a situation. While reading his Bible, he came upon the phrase "Leave room for God's wrath" (Romans 12:19). The context of the phrase is that we shouldn't try to get even when someone harms us, but instead leave room for God to settle the score.

If we can leave room for God's anger, Morgan reasoned, "Can we not, when facing other challenges, leave room for His other attributes? For His power? For His grace? For His intervention?" Morgan relates, "I underlined the words *leave room for God* and have leaned on them ever since."[1]

In the epic movie *The Ten Commandments*, the most famous scene was when the Israelites were facing the Red Sea, trapped by mountains on both sides and the Egyptian army in pursuit. God parted the Red Sea so that the Israelites could cross on dry land to safety.

Like the Israelites you may be trapped by your circumstances. The Red Sea of Sure Disaster is in front of you. The Mountains of Impossibility shut you in on both sides, and Certain Calamity is coming closer and closer. Friend, leave room for God. He still knows how to part the Red Sea.

Today may be the very day God rescues you. Moses told the Israelites, "Do not be afraid. Stand firm and you will see the deliverance the LORD will bring you today. . . . The LORD will fight for you; you need only to be still" (Exodus 14:13–14).

Just wait a little longer. Leave room for God to act.

[1]Robert J. Morgan, *The Red Sea Rules* (Nashville, TN: Thomas Nelson, Inc., 2001), 50.

61

*There will be no more night. They will not need the light of
a lamp or the light of the sun, for the Lord God will give
them light. And they will reign for ever and ever.*

REVELATION 22:5

I NEED SHADES

Strolling through the mall, I caught sight of a T-shirt with the catchy slogan: "The future is so bright, I need shades."

I couldn't help smiling. In fact, as I continued walking, my whole attitude lightened. Jesus is my Savior and heaven is my home. No matter how gloomy the present is, the future is bright—very bright. One day, when all the problems of this life are over, I'll spend forever with the Lord. What could be more hopeful?

I'm sure that if we could get even a glimpse into heaven, our human eyes would need heavy-duty sunglasses because of the light. The last book of the Bible tells us, "There will be no more night. They will not need the light of a lamp or the light of the sun, for the Lord God will give them light" (Revelation 22:5).

But instead of focusing on the bright future, I tend to focus on the depressing problem I'm dealing with right now. I need to put on the sunglasses of faith and look forward to the future with expectancy.

Jesus mastered that principle. He Himself exemplified forward-looking faith. The Bible tells us for the joy that was set before Him, Jesus endured death by crucifixion (Hebrews 12:2). He bore the darkness of Calvary and its excruciating pain because He knew the light that awaited Him in His Father's presence. We can keep going the same way—enduring pain because of joy ahead.

If life is bleak, turn to Jesus, the Light of the world. Then look ahead, for the future is as bright as the promises of God. You may even want to get yourself one of those T-shirts.

62

For we know that our old self was crucified with him
so that the body ruled by sin might be done away with,
that we should no longer be slaves to sin.

ROMANS 6:6

(THE WHOLE STORY: ROMANS 6:6–7, 11)

A BRAND-NEW BEGINNING

Is your past keeping you from being your best right now, in the present? Past sins do that, you know. David Eckman writes,

> *Sin walks us into a huge warehouse filled with video clips of*
> *us and says, "This is your life. We have thousands of clips of*
> *your failures. Many of them are so embarrassing. . . . That is*
> *all you are, and we have the record of it. So you might as well*
> *surrender to sin within, because you can't be better than this.*
> *You are these [video] clips—and nothing else."*[1]

Perhaps you are convinced that your past is who you are, and you can't change. There's good news; "Jesus has burned the warehouse!"[2]

The Bible tells us,

For we know that our old self was crucified with him so that the body ruled by sin might be done away with, that we should no longer be slaves to sin—because anyone who has died has been set free from sin. . . . In the same way, count yourselves dead to sin but alive to God in Christ Jesus.
ROMANS 6:6–7, 11

Those video clips are a true picture of your past, no doubt about it. But Jesus paid the penalty that justice demands for your sins. When you accept God's forgiveness, it's as if you died and rose again to a new life. And that's where God wants you to live—in the present, not the past.

As a Christian, you are not the sum total of your past. You are a brand-new person with a brand-new beginning.

[1]David Eckman, *Becoming Who God Intended* (Eugene, OR: Harvest House Publishers, 2005), 153.
[2]Ibid.

63

My flesh and my heart may fail, but God is the strength of my heart and my portion forever.

PSALM 73:26

WHEN YOUR HUT'S ON FIRE

The scraggly man had been washed ashore a small, uninhabited island—the sole survivor of a shipwreck. Every day he prayed feverishly for God to rescue him. And every day he scanned the horizon for help, but to no avail. Eventually he managed to build a little hut out of driftwood where he stored his few possessions and got some protection from the sun. At least now he had a place to call "home."

One day, after scavenging for food, he arrived back to find his little hut in flames, smoke rolling up to the sky. Stunned with disbelief and anger, he lifted his face to the sky and cried, "God! How could You do this to me?!"

After a fitful sleep on the sand, he was awakened by the sound of a ship that had come to rescue him.

"How did you know I was here?" the weary man asked his rescuers.

"We saw your smoke signal," they replied.[1] You too may be distraught with the way things are going in your life. Shipwrecked, with your hut burning, everything you treasure seems gone. Your source of security—whether possessions or a person you depend on—has been taken from you. But, friend, remember you still have God. And He knows where you are. Don't lose heart. Your "burning hut" may be used by Him to signal help from a source you never thought would come to your rescue.

Many times the writer of the Psalms despaired of any human help. Yet he knew he could count on God. He wrote, "My flesh and my heart may fail, but God is the strength of my heart and my portion forever" (Psalm 73:26). Hang on until help comes.

[1]http://intentional-christian.org/?p=221, accessed May 1, 2008, author unknown.

64

But I have calmed and quieted myself, I am like a weaned child with its mother; like a weaned child I am content.

PSALM 131:2

SATISFIED

For a long time now I've been fascinated with Psalm 131:2: "I have calmed and quieted myself, I am like a weaned child with its mother; like a weaned child I am content." Why did the psalmist choose the comparison of a weaned child to the peace and quiet he was experiencing in his heart?

I found the answer when I thought about my three kids. When they were tiny babies they were eager to be near me when they were hungry. But by the time they were toddlers, they would just sit quietly on my lap because they had been weaned.

Many of us are like needy newborn babies. Every time we pray, we want something from God, immediately. Of course, He doesn't mind us drawing near to Him. But I can't help thinking He would be pleased if sometimes we would come into His presence just for the joy of closeness.

Wawa Ponce came to God with a need. She wanted a husband. Sad that God had not yet met that yearning, her deep longing was almost a physical pain. Then God led her to Psalm 131:2 and the image of a young child peacefully cradled in her mother's arms—so quiet, so still. Wawa wrote:

I want to be that child. No, I need to be that child. I need God to wean me from what I want, to prepare me for what He wants for me. I need to be still in His arms knowing that He would take care of my needs—even my wants.[1]

Then she concluded with a prayer of acceptance: "Lord, I will wait and be satisfied with Your answer." And peace came.

Have you quieted your soul? You can find peace and satisfaction in God's arms.

[1]Wawa Ponce, "Weaning Love" in *Women on the Journey: Defining Moments,* compiled and edited by Michelle Ocampo-Joaquin (Makati City, Philippines: Church Strengthening Ministry, Inc., 2004), 173.

65

Cast all your anxiety on
him because he cares for you.

1 Peter 5:7

Practical Atheism

One time, Jesus said to a busy woman, "Martha, Martha, you are anxious and troubled about many things" (Luke 10:41 ESV). I can certainly relate to Martha. If you're like most women, you don't worry about just one thing. Because we're good at multitasking, we're usually anxious about a *collection* of things.

I did a search in the New Testament on the word *anxious* and discovered that every time the word is used, it's connected to our concern with what *we* are going to do about a situation—what we're going to say or do or wear or eat or whatever. I don't worry about whether the earth is going to keep turning on its axis. I worry about me—my needs, my health, my family, my work.

Are you worried? What do you think about this statement: "All anxiety is practical atheism"? I find it startling, for it means that when we are anxious and worried, we're living as if there were no God.

You may believe there is a God, but maybe you think solving your problems is *your* responsibility—you got yourself into this mess, so it's up to you to get yourself out of it. Or perhaps God seems remote, and you ask, "Does He really care about me?" So you carry a heart-heavy load of anxiety.

What we need to do when we're anxious is to stop being "practical atheists" and turn to the Lord. God is big enough to solve any problem. Peter tells us, "Cast all your anxiety on him because he cares for you" (1 Peter 5:7).

66

"Before long, the world will not see me anymore,
but you will see me. Because I live, you also will live."

JOHN 14:19

THE LAND OF THE DYING

In his later years, pastor and Christian statesman Dr. D. James Kennedy wrote:

> *I know that someday I am going to come to what some*
> *people will say is the end of this life. . . . I don't want them*
> *to cry. I want them to begin the [memorial] service with the*
> *Doxology and end with the Hallelujah chorus, because. . .*
> *I am not going to be dead. I will be more alive than I have*
> *ever been in my life, and I will be looking down upon you*
> *poor people who are still in the land of the dying and have*
> *not yet joined me in the land of the living. And I will be*
> *alive forevermore.*[1]

Life on earth is often referred to as the "land of the living," but as Dr. Kennedy says, it's really the "land of the dying." If you are God's child, one day you will be in heaven, the true "land of the living." It was Jesus Himself who, after He was resurrected, said, "Because I live, you also will live" (John 14:19).

Are you certain that someday you're going to be in heaven? You can be. Romans 10:9 tells us, "If you declare with your mouth, 'Jesus is Lord,' and believe in your heart that God raised him from the dead, you will be saved."

When you take those two steps— confess Jesus as Lord and believe He rose from the dead—the Spirit of God comes to live within you. Then you know where you'll spend eternity.

Someday we'll say goodbye to the "land of the dying" and start Life with a capital *L* in the "land of the living." Meet me there.

67

*About midnight Paul and Silas were praying and singing hymns
to God, and the other prisoners were listening to them. Suddenly
there was such a violent earthquake that the foundations of
the prison were shaken. At once all the prison doors flew
open, and everyone's chains came loose.*

ACTS 16:25–26
(THE WHOLE STORY: ACTS 16:16–34)

SINGING IN THE DARK

Dark periods in life come to us all, times when we feel as if
we are in a prison cell and all we know about God is put to
the test. The apostle Paul had an experience like that when
he and Silas arrived in Philippi. As a result of casting an evil
spirit out of a slave girl so that she could no longer foretell the
future and make money for her owners, the two were severely
beaten and put in prison.

So here they are chained to a wall in total darkness with bloody, stinging backs. But instead of wallowing in self-pity, they rejoiced. "About midnight Paul and Silas were praying and singing hymns to God" (Acts 16:25). Amazing!

Then another amazing thing happened. A violent earthquake shook the prison so strongly that all the prison doors flew open and the prisoners' chains came loose. In the next few hours Paul and Silas led their jailer to faith in Jesus. The jailer washed their wounds and fed them in his home. Afterward, Paul and Silas baptized him, along with all his family.

Do your circumstances feel like a prison cell from which there is no escape? Does darkness surround you and are you in pain? Hold on to the unshakeable truths about God—He is all powerful, all knowing, and all loving. Do what Paul and Silas did—pray and sing hymns and worship songs to the Lord in the dark until He sends the earthquake that will release you from your cell. As Pastor Buddy Owens puts it, "Don't allow prison to shake your faith; let faith shake your prison."

68

Your beauty. . .should be that of your inner self,
the unfading beauty of a gentle and quiet spirit,
which is of great worth in God's sight.

1 PETER 3:3–4

QUIET TIME

Author Elizabeth George writes,

> *If someone asked you to describe the quiet time you had this*
> *morning, what would you say? This is exactly the question*
> *Dawson Trotman, founder of The Navigators ministry*
> *organization, used to ask men and women applying for mis-*
> *sions work. . . . He spent a half hour with each one, asking*
> *specifically about their devotional life. Sadly, only one person*
> *out of twenty-nine interviewed said his devotional life was*
> *a constant in his life.*[1]

You may be thinking, *Of course, people in full-time Christian ministry should be having a quiet time.* But you might be surprised to learn how few people in ministry regularly do take time to not only talk to God but let God talk to them. Before we get too critical of them, let's evaluate our own quiet time.

Many of us think we're doing God a favor by talking to Him, when it's really incredible we have that privilege at all. We're the losers if we carry a load of worry instead of bringing it to our Savior, who loves us so. I like the way Corrie ten Boom puts it: "As a camel kneels before his master to have him remove his burden, so kneel and let the Master take your burden."[2] It's worth giving up some sleep to have intimate time with Him.

Quiet time with the Lord will give us a quiet spirit, which is an "unfading beauty…of great worth in God's sight" (1 Peter 3:4). Don't miss this special time. It's better for us than any trip to the spa!

[1]Elizabeth George, *A Woman After God's Own Heart* (Eugene, OR: Harvest House Publishers, 1997), 30.
[2]Corrie ten Boom, *Don't Wrestle, Just Nestle* (Old Tappan, NJ: Revell, 1978), 79.

69

The righteous perish, and no one takes it to heart; the devout are taken away, and no one understands that the righteous are taken away to be spared from evil. Those who walk uprightly enter into peace; they find rest as they lie in death.

ISAIAH 57:1–2

SPARED FROM EVIL

Why do good people die while evil men continue to live and thrive? For example, why is a fine Christian killed in an auto accident while the drunk who hit him walks away uninjured?

I found a verse in the Bible that gives insight: "The righteous perish, and no one takes it to heart; the devout are taken away, and no one understands that the righteous are taken away to be spared from evil" (Isaiah 57:1). That means when a Christian dies, perhaps at a young age, it may be because God took him home to spare him from a difficult situation he would have had to face if he had lived longer.

My parents lived to be eighty-nine and ninety-two—long, full lives. After my dad went to be with the Lord, the last church where he was pastor veered from the direction of his leadership, and big problems developed. The congregation dwindled drastically. Many a time I prayed, "Thank You, thank You, Lord, for taking him home so that he didn't have to see this happening." It would have broken his heart, for he truly loved the people in his congregation. It was at that point that I understood that God had taken my dad away "to be spared from evil."

I'm so glad believers in heaven don't know the sad things that happen on earth, for the Bible tells us God wipes " 'every tear from their eyes. There will be no more death' or mourning or crying or pain" (Revelation 21:4), and "Those who walk uprightly enter into peace; they find rest as they lie in death" (Isaiah 57:2)—spared at last from all evil. Thank You, Lord!

70

He will cover you with his feathers,
and under his wings you will find refuge;
his faithfulness will be your shield and rampart.

PSALM 91:4

WHEN YOU FEEL LIKE HIDING

Sometimes I just want to be invisible. I don't want to hear anyone call my name, or ask me a question, or expect anything from me. I just want to hide somewhere where no one can find me. Do you know the feeling? Do you ever wish you could just stay in bed and pull the covers over your head for the entire day?

Few of us have that luxury. People are depending on us. Husbands and children need our care. We can't risk losing our jobs or neglecting our households. So we keep going.

There is one place, however, where we *can* go to hide. We can run to God, as a baby bird runs to its mother. Psalm 91 tells us: "He will cover you with his feathers, and under his wings you will find refuge" (Psalm 91:4).

For a baby bird, being under its mother's wings is being close to the one who takes care of its needs. For us, being under God's wings means safety, comfort, and provision.

If you're feeling tired and overstretched, may these verses give you rest:

- The psalmist David wrote, "In peace I will lie down and sleep, for you alone, LORD, make me dwell in safety" (Psalm 4:8).

- God says, "As a mother comforts her child, so will I comfort you" (Isaiah 66:13).

- The apostle Paul wrote, "And God is able to bless you abundantly, so that in all things at all times, having all that you need, you will abound in every good work" (2 Corinthians 9:8).

Under God's wings, we know He comforts and protects us. Run to Him when you feel like hiding.

71

But now he has reconciled you by Christ's physical body
through death to present you holy in his sight,
without blemish and free from accusation.

COLOSSIANS 1:22

HE WANTS US

Imagine being able to have anything you want—anything. You could just "speak it" and it would be in existence. That's how it is with God. He can create anything He desires. And He did.

What amazes me is that He created *us*, knowing that the free will He gave us would result in our rejecting Him and choosing our own way. Why? As incredible as it may be, God created us because He wants to have a relationship with us.

But there was a tremendous cost to this plan. God would have to redeem us from our fallen or sinful condition so that He—a holy God—could have fellowship with us.

The price was the death of His Son, Jesus, on the cross. The Bible tells us, "But now he has reconciled you by Christ's physical body through death to present you holy in his sight, without blemish and free from accusation" (Colossians 1:22). What a price for God! What a miracle for us!

He did all this because He wants us for Himself.

> But now, this is what the LORD says—
> he who created you, Jacob,
> he who formed you, Israel:
> "Do not fear, for I have redeemed you;
> I have summoned you by name; you are mine."
> ISAIAH 43:1

We are His! He wants us! In spite of all our "warts" and imperfections and limitations, He wants us! What a magnificent truth! Thank You, thank You, Lord!

72

But the Lord has become my fortress,
and my God the rock in whom I take refuge.

Psalm 94:22

SAYING GOODBYE

When my uncle Phil passed away from cancer, it was very difficult for my aunt Margaret, for they had been so happily married for nearly sixty years. They had done everything together.

The following year, Margaret's friend watched her husband also lose the battle to cancer. Knowing the agony of losing one's spouse, Margaret wrote to her:

I remember those days. They are hard. You know what is happening, but it seems unreal because you are still living daily life. And you survive by doing just that—living daily life.

While Ralph is here, give and receive lots of hugs and kisses, remember together lots of good experiences, say everything you need to say. [Phil and I] always knew we were good partners and we spoke of it often, thanking God. Now I wish I had looked him in the eyes a few more times and said very clearly to him, "You have been a wonderful husband."

Before he died, twice Phil asked me if I would be okay. I replied, "I won't like it one bit. But I will be okay. The Lord and the girls will take care of me." And that has proven to be true.

I will be praying as you offer your precious one to the Lord with thanksgiving and praise. It is just one step at a time. A cup of tea or coffee. A pat on the cheek. A kiss. A smile and a tease. Just live now. Don't think about what is next. When you get to "next," God will still be there.

Margaret has come to realize that even though the person closest to her heart is gone, the Lord is still with her. She has proven to be true what the psalmist wrote: "But the LORD has become my fortress, and my God the rock in whom I take refuge" (Psalm 94:22).

73

*"Such is the destiny of all who forget God; so perishes
the hope of the godless. What they trust in is fragile;
what they rely on is a spider's web. They lean on the web,
but it gives way; they cling to it, but it does not hold."*

JOB 8:13–15

RELYING ON A SPIDER'S WEB

The book of Job includes a very interesting picture of the person
who forgets God in his life.

> *"Such is the destiny of all who forget God. . . .
> What they trust in is fragile;
> what they rely on is a spider's web.
> They lean on the web, but it gives way;
> they cling to it, but it does not hold."*

JOB 8:13–15

No security there! While a spider's web is actually very strong for a spider's weight, it is no match for the weight of a human being. Neither is anything else worth relying on except God. Nothing else will hold up.

Paul learned this. Telling of the hardships he experienced in Asia, he wrote:

We were under great pressure, far beyond our ability to endure, so that we despaired of life itself. Indeed, we felt we had received the sentence of death. But this happened that we might not rely on ourselves but on God, who raises the dead. He has delivered us from such a deadly peril, and he will deliver us again. On him we have set our hope that he will continue to deliver us.
2 CORINTHIANS 1:8–10

No spider webs for Paul! Because of his intense circumstances, he knew he needed to rely on God. And so do we.

The God we can rely on is no weak, frail God. Moses exclaimed, "Sovereign LORD. . .what god is there in heaven or on earth who can do the deeds and mighty works you do?" (Deuteronomy 3:24). When the winds are raging in your life, hold on to Him. Much stronger than a spider's web, God's arms will never let you down.

74

It is good to praise the LORD and make music to your name,
O Most High, proclaiming your love in the morning
and your faithfulness at night.

PSALM 92:1–2

praise: A.M. anD P.M.

Did you notice these verses tell us how to pray in the morning
and how to pray at night?

A.M.: Start your day by declaring His love. Doing this will
put your day in perspective. I, for one, need that first thing in
the morning. When we think about how much God loves us,
we want to use the day wisely. The Bible says, "He died for all,
that those who live should no longer live for themselves but
for him who died for them" (2 Corinthians 5:15). Living for
Christ is life in its highest form. Living for ourselves brings
neither happiness nor significance.

154

Remembering how much God loves you will help you whether the day goes as you planned or is total chaos. If your boss questions your work, you still know that the Lord loves you and values you. If your teen ignores you, you still know God cares.

P.M.: Thank Him for His faithfulness—another day of good health, money to pay the bills, safety as you went to work. If your day held pain and disappointment, thank Him still, for He was faithful and got you through the day. Even Jesus said, "I must press on today and tomorrow and the next day" (Luke 13:33).

Not a day goes by that we have nothing for which to praise the Lord. The psalmist David said, "Every day I will praise you and extol your name for ever and ever" (Psalm 145:2).

75

"My yoke is easy and my burden is light."
MATTHEW 11:30

crazy love

Pastor Francis Chan says that we're missing something important when we look at our relationship with God as a chore, a sacrifice. He writes. "What we need is to be consumed… to be *obsessed*—with nothing and no one else but God."[1] When we love Him that intensely, says Chan, we will find that His commands are easy to obey instead of an unpleasant duty. The following allegory illustrates this truth.

Alex was an outstanding young man—handsome, with a good job, a born athlete, and a leader. Naturally, girls were attracted to Alex, and he thought they were pretty special as well.

On Monday night Alex took Emily out. On Tuesday, he took Chelsea out. On Wednesday, it was Christine—every night a different girl. After a while, however, a special girl named Grace came along, and Alex fell in love with her.

Monday night it was Grace; Tuesday it was Grace; Wednesday, Thursday, Friday—he was with her all the time.

Alex's friend said, "Poor Alex! It's just Grace, morning, noon, and night!"

Alex said, "Look, don't feel bad for me. I love Grace, and I want to be with her every day."

When you really love Jesus, it's going to be easier when God says no to the Emilys and Chelseas of this world, for when you are in love with Him, you know who truly matters. When we are "crazy" about Him, we will understand the truth of Jesus' words, "my yoke is easy and my burden is light" (Matthew 11:30).

[1]Frances Chan with Danae Yankoski, *Crazy Love*, http://www.christianbooksummaries.com/archive.php?v=4&i=19, excerpted by *Christian Book Summaries*, Vol 4, Issue 19, summarized by Kristyn Chiapperino, July 2008, 7

76

*"My Father's house has many rooms; if that were not so, would
I have told you that I am going there to prepare a place for you?
And if I go and prepare a place for you, I will come back and
take you to be with me that you also may be where I am."*

JOHN 14:2–3

I WILL COME BACK FOR YOU

Have you seen the look of uncertainty in the eyes of a toddler
when his mom leaves him with a friend or relative for a few
hours? She assures him, "Don't worry, in just a little while I
will be back for you."

I'm so glad Jesus also assured us that He will come back
for us. Just before He died, He told us, "My Father's house
has many rooms; if that were not so, would I have told you
that I am going there to prepare a place for you? And if I go
and prepare a place for you, I will come back and take you to
be with me that you also may be where I am" (John 14:2–3).

What a comfort these words are when life is tough! When your world falls apart, focus on the reality that this life is not the end. Author Max Lucado writes,

> [Jesus] pledges to take us home. He does not delegate this task. He may send missionaries to teach you, angels to protect you, teachers to guide you, singers to inspire you, and physicians to heal you, but He sends no one to take you. He reserves this job for Himself. "I will come back and take you home."[1]

I like that. Just the thought that one day Jesus will personally come back for me to take me to be with Him in His house forever gives me courage to wade through the muck that life brings. May you too say with conviction the concluding words of the familiar Psalm 23, "I will dwell in the house of the LORD forever." At the end of life's day, your Shepherd will be there to lead you home.

[1]Max Lucado, *Traveling Light* (Nashville, TN: W Publishing Group, 2001), 84–85.

77

This is how we know what love is: Jesus Christ laid down his life for us. And we ought to lay down our lives for our brothers and sisters.

1 John 3:16

WHAT CAN I GIVE HIM?

You don't have to think very long about Christ's sacrifice for you before you feel a profound sense of debt for what He did. As the apostle John wrote, "This is how we know what love is: Jesus Christ laid down his life for us" (1 John 3:16).

Hymn writer Isaac Watts, who penned the words to "When I Survey the Wondrous Cross," so beautifully expressed the immensity of God's gift:

Were the whole realm of nature mine,
That were an offering far too small;
Love so amazing, so divine,
Demands my soul, my life, my all.

If we owned all the galaxies in the universe to give to God in appreciation, it would be, as Watts puts it, a gift "far too small." The only thing we actually possess to give God is ourselves: "Love so amazing, so divine, demands my soul, my life, my all."

When we sang this hymn when I was a child, we would repeat the last line with one slight change: "Love so amazing, so divine, *shall have* my soul, my life, my all." That always sent a shiver up and down my spine. Even at that young age I wanted God to have just that—my all.

Don't think I haven't had trouble keeping that commitment! My selfish nature wants to renege and take back control. But the good news is we can make that dedication anew every morning. We can pray, "Lord, today, I want You to have all my day, my energy, my devotion in response to Your great love for me." It's the only way I know to say, "Thank You."

78

*You will keep in perfect peace those whose
minds are steadfast, because they trust in you.*

ISAIAH 26:3

S F G T D

Perhaps someone has emailed you this memo:

*This is God. Today I will be handling all of your problems
for you. I do not need your help. So, have a nice day. I love
you.*

*P.S. And, remember. . . If life happens to deliver a
situation to you that you cannot handle, do not attempt
to resolve it yourself! Kindly put it in the SFGTD
(Something-for-God-to-Do) Box. All situations will be
resolved in My time, not yours.*

*Once the matter is placed into the box, do not hold on to
it by worrying about it. Instead, focus on all the wonderful
things that are present in your life now.*

Do you have a Something-for-God-to-Do Box? It's a splendid idea for those times when you just can't stop worrying about a problem close to your heart. It is much better to *do* something with your worry. First, tell the Lord about it. Then decisively put your worry in an SFGTD Box.

Of course, this box has no lid, so it's very easy to reach inside, take your worry out, and—well, worry about it some more. Adopt a hands-off policy and trust God. The prophet Isaiah wrote, "You will keep in perfect peace him whose mind is steadfast, because he trusts in you" (Isaiah 26:3).

To trust God does not imply that you are neglectful. On the contrary, trusting Him means that you are choosing His solution. You are simply telling God, "I believe You are a good God who wants the very best for me, and I am choosing to leave the problem in Your hands to answer in Your time and Your way." I think you will be surprised at the peace that fills your heart.

79

"Very truly I tell you, whoever hears my word and believes him who sent me has eternal life and will not be judged but has crossed over from death to life."

JOHN 5:24

ETERNITY

Eternity—time without beginning or end! St. Augustine, one of the early church fathers, wrote:

It is hard for us who are bounded by time to glimpse eternity in all its splendor. . . . Eternity is supreme since it is a never-ending present. You are before all past time and after all future time, O God Almighty. Your knowledge is far more wonderful and mysterious than we can imagine.[1]

Trying to think of eternity is frustrating because everything that we have ever known—except God—has existed in time. John Bate, whose writings inspired Isaac Newton's scientific investigations, tells the story: " 'What is eternity?' was a question once asked at the deaf and dumb institution in Paris, and the beautiful and striking answer was given by one of the pupils, 'The lifetime of the Almighty.'"[2]

Hymn writer Reginald Heber wrote, "Eternity has no gray hairs!"[3] I like that! For me nothing explains eternity in a form I can understand as well as the final verse of John Newton's beloved hymn "Amazing Grace."

> *When we've been here ten thousand years*
> *Bright shining as the sun,*
> *We've no less days to sing God's praise*
> *Than when we've first begun.*

The joys of eternal life begin not when we die but from the day we begin a relationship with Jesus. He said, "Very truly I tell you, whoever hears my word and believes him who sent me has eternal life and will not be judged but has crossed over from death to life" (John 5:24). Eternity is forever. Are you ready?

---

[1]St. Augustine of Hippo, *Confessions* (from the Classics Collection, Volume 3, Issue 35, August 2007, ChristianBookSummaries.com, summarized by Wendy Connell), 7.
[2]http://www.giga-usa.com/quotes/topics/eternity_t001.htm, accessed October 17, 2008.
[3]Ibid.

80

May the God of hope fill you with all joy
and peace as you trust in him...

ROMANS 15:13

LET GO

My friend who is fighting cancer sent me a helpful news-letter from the support group The Cancer Connection.[1] Following are excerpts:

> *One of the hardest things we have to learn to do in this life is to "let go." Especially as we see things that we want to fix....*
>
> *This compulsion to "do something!" can become mad-dening when we are faced with cancer.*
>
> *The best advice we have ever received is to do what we can in terms of caring for ourselves and caring for others who need us but not to the point of exhausting ourselves. After these things, let go. Surrender whatever your cares and worries are to [God].[2]*

Robert J. Burdette's poem "Broken Dreams" tells of the trouble of not letting go.

> As children bring their broken toys
> With tears for us to mend,
> I brought my broken dreams to God
> Because He was my friend.
>
> But then instead of leaving Him
> In peace to work alone,
> I hung around and tried to help
> With ways that were my own.
>
> At last I snatched them back and cried,
> "How could you be so slow?"
> "My child," He said, "what could I do?
> You never did let go."

Are you suffering from a serious illness? "May the God of hope fill you with all joy and peace as you trust in him, so that you may overflow with hope by the power of the Holy Spirit" (Romans 15:13).

[1]Because the editor uses "whatever Higher Power you believe in" for "God" to appeal to all faiths, I have taken the liberty to insert the name of the only One who can truly help us, our heavenly Father.
[2]July 2008 Newsletter of "The Cancer Connection," www.thecancercrusade.com.

81

"I, even I, am he who blots out your transgressions,
for my own sake, and remembers your sins no more."

ISAIAH 43:25

GOD FORGETS

Mention any date since 1980 to Jill Price, and she can tell you what happened to her on that day—"Who[m] she met, what she did, what she ate. In effect, she is a human diary."[1]

The problem is that Jill can remember every mistake she ever made as if it had just happened. "Most have called it a gift. But I call it a burden," she says. "I recall every bad decision, insult, and excruciating embarrassment. Over the years it has eaten me up. It has kind of paralyzed me."[2]

Can you imagine how painful it would be to remember the intricate details of everything you had ever done wrong? It would be a nightmare.

Even though we don't have Jill Price's memory, we do generally remember for a very long time what we've done wrong. In contrast to ours, however, God's memory works differently. Yes, He is all knowing but the Bible tells us that when He forgives our sins, at that point, He chooses to forget them completely. God says, "I, even I, am he who blots out your transgressions. . .and remembers your sins no more" (Isaiah 43:25). Those sins can never be brought against us for all eternity.

Are you living with a load of guilt because of what you've done in the past? If you have asked God to forgive you, those sins are gone—forgotten by God. So, why don't you let them go too, and enjoy His gift of grace today.

[1]Barry Wigmore, "The Woman Who Can't Forget Anything," May 8, 2008, http://www.dailymail.co.uk/news/article-564948/The-woman-forget-ANYTHINGWidow-ability—curse—perfectly-remember-single-day-life.html, accessed October 17, 2008.
[2]Ibid.

82

*And we all, who with unveiled faces contemplate
the Lord's glory, are being transformed into his image
with ever-increasing glory, which comes
from the Lord, who is the Spirit.*

2 CORINTHIANS 3:18

your face

Do you like your picture on your ID card? Probably not. But you're stuck with it, right?

Most of us are not satisfied with how we look, so we go to a lot of trouble to make our faces look as good as possible. Stores carry products claiming to help us look younger, prettier, and healthier. In the US alone, $18.8 billion is spent annually on cosmetics.[1]

Let's face it, people sometimes judge us by how we look. But not even the best cosmetic can mask the emotions our faces reveal—joy, anger, peace. Because we women easily pick up the signals, we read people's faces to see what is going on in their minds.

For followers of Christ, the apostle Paul declares, "We all, who with unveiled faces contemplate the Lord's glory, are being transformed into his image with ever-increasing glory, which comes from the Lord, who is the Spirit" (2 Corinthians 3:18).

The picture Paul paints is that when we focus on the Lord, we become more like Him. The better we know Him, the more we reflect Him to others as light reflected by a mirror makes a face glow. The wonder is that in the process of learning to know the Lord, we are changed into His likeness by the Holy Spirit. Now, that is true beauty!

Mrs. Wang stands out in my memory for the glow of God's presence on her face. Her husband, Wang Ming-Dao, was the "father" of the house church movement in China. Because she was a Christian she spent twenty hard years in prison. Yet when I met her, I saw no bitterness—only the love of the Lord in her face.

The more closely we follow Christ, the more we will be like Him.

[1]http://www.crescatsententia.net/archives/2003/12/10/, accessed July 1, 2008.

83

Whoever fears the L ord has a secure fortress,
and for their children it will be a refuge.

Proverbs 14:26

Always on the Job

Dorothy Nicholas and her husband were talking to their next-door neighbors, a young couple who had helped them on many occasions.

Out of the blue, the neighbor began to tell them of his difficult past. As a teen growing up in Greenwood, South Carolina, he had become involved with the wrong crowd and ended up spending a year in juvenile prison. When he was released, he had problems finding a job.

In desperation, he decided to rob a gas station to get enough money to leave South Carolina. He stole his father's car and gun and drove to a local station before closing time. He was about to demand all the money from the woman manager when he looked up and saw a sign over the service window that read, GOD IS OUR SECURITY GUARD—ALWAYS ON THE JOB. Suddenly he realized he just couldn't rob that place. Guilt-laden, he rushed home and prayed all night, asking for forgiveness and courage to go right. And with God's help, he did.

Hearing the story, Dorothy looked at her husband. Both were thinking of a night thirteen years earlier in that same town of Greenwood when they worked on ideas for a sign for their business. Finally the right words came. The slogan Dorothy's husband put on the sign at the small gas station they managed was this: GOD IS OUR SECURITY GUARD—ALWAYS ON THE JOB.[1]

Yes, God was truly "on the job" that night—and always will be. Psalm 121 says, "He will not let your foot slip—he who watches over you will not slumber" (Psalm 121:3). Your greatest security rests in God.

---

[1]Elizabeth Sherrill, *His Mysterious Ways*, vol. 2, compiled by the Editors (Carmel, NY: Guideposts Associates, Inc., 1991), 12–13.

84

"Surely I am with you always,
to the very end of the age."

MATTHEW 28:20

(THE WHOLE STORY: MATTHEW 28:18–20)

THE WORD OF A GENTLEMAN

In 1865, David Livingstone, renowned missionary and explorer in Africa, had to pass through land controlled by a chief who had aggressively been opposing his work. Livingstone was warned that warriors were in the jungle ahead creeping toward his camp.

Going alone to his tent, Livingstone opened his Bible to Matthew 28:18–20. Then he wrote the following in his journal:

January 14, 1856. Felt much turmoil of spirit in view of having all my plans for the welfare of this great region and teeming population knocked on the head by savages tomorrow. But I read that Jesus came and said, "All Power is given unto Me in Heaven and in Earth. Go ye therefore, and teach all nations. . .and lo, I am with you always, even unto the end of the world." It's the word of a Gentleman of the most sacred and strictest honour, and there's an end on it! I will not cross furtively by night. . . . I feel quite calm now, thank God![1]

The next morning, while the chief and his men watched from the jungle's edge, Livingstone instructed the expedition to cross the river. He deliberately chose to be in the last seat in the last canoe, making himself vulnerable to attack.

"Tell [the chief] to observe that I am not afraid,"[2] said Livingstone, never looking back. The entire group crossed safely. God kept His word.

In the uncertainty of your circumstances, you too can hold on to God's promise to be with you always. You have the word of a Gentleman.

[1] I. Schapera, ed., *Livingstone's African Journal 1853–1856*, 2 vols. (London: Chatto and Windus, 1963), 2: 374.
[2] Ibid.

85

*He tends his flock like a shepherd: He gathers
the lambs in his arms and carries them close to
his heart; he gently leads those that have young.*

ISAIAH 40:11

GOD'S COMPASSIONATE HEART

You've probably heard the saying, "People don't care how much you know—until they know how much you care." It's true, isn't it?

Let's say that I have a problem with my computer. No matter how hard I try, I can't fix it. As I sit in front of a blank screen increasingly frustrated, along comes a guy who has a degree in computer science. He stops at my desk and looks at what I'm doing. Almost immediately he figures out the problem. He tells me what is wrong—and then walks off, leaving me to continue my struggle. I'm more frustrated than ever! This guy knows what the problem is but he doesn't care enough to help me. He only wants me to know how smart he is.

I'm so glad that God is not like that. He who has all knowledge also has all compassion. He deeply cares for us. The prophet Isaiah pictured Him as a tender shepherd who looks after His flock: "He gathers the lambs in his arms and carries them close to his heart; he gently leads those that have young" (Isaiah 40:11).

When Jesus was here on earth, "he saw the crowds, [and] he had compassion on them, because they were harassed and helpless, like sheep without a shepherd" (Matthew 9:36).

Friend, I hope you will think of God not only as the One who knows all about you but also the One who cares for you more than any other does. God not only knows the facts of your situation, but He also sympathizes with you. He cares. Find comfort today in His love. Let Him hold you close to His heart.

86

I was shown mercy so that in me, the worst of sinners, Christ Jesus might display his immense patience as an example for those who would believe in him and receive eternal life.

1 Timothy 1:16

Pretty Enough for God to Love You

Amy was delighted to discover a beautiful doll under the Christmas tree. Clasping her lovely new doll, she hurried to hug her grandmother, who had given it to her. "Thank you, thank you," she cried.

All day long Amy played with her new doll. But toward the end of the day, her grandma noticed she was cuddling her old doll—the one that was ragged and missing one eye.

"It seems, Amy, that you like that old doll better than your new one," her grandmother commented.

"Oh Grandma, I like my new doll so much," Amy rushed to assure her. "But I love this old doll more, because if I didn't love her, no one else would."[1]

Perhaps you are like the beautiful new doll—everyone likes you because you are so lovely. Thank God for His special gift to you and use it wisely to make good friends and brighten the lives of others.

But maybe you feel more like the other doll—worn out, used, not pretty or special. Be encouraged that God loves you every bit as much as He loves the seemingly more gifted person. Just as Amy loved both of her dolls, so God loves you just as you are. He won't fling you aside.

The apostle Paul, before becoming a believer, had persecuted Christians. He wrote: "I was shown mercy so that in me, the worst of sinners, Christ Jesus might display his immense patience as an example for those who would believe in him and receive eternal life" (1 Timothy 1:16).

Rest in the arms of the One who loves you with unconditional love.

---

[1] *God's Little Devotional Book for Women* (Tulsa, OK: Honor Books, Inc., 1996), 235.

87

For to us a child is born, to us a son is given, and the government will be on his shoulders. And he will be called Wonderful Counselor, Mighty God, Everlasting Father, Prince of Peace.

ISAIAH 9:6

ALL YOU NEED

Sometimes Bible verses become so familiar we gloss over them without seeing how they apply in a practical way to our lives. Isaiah 9:6 is one of those:

For to us a child is born,
to us a son is given,
and the government will be on his shoulders.
And he will be called
Wonderful Counselor, Mighty God,
Everlasting Father, Prince of Peace.

We generally assign that verse to the Christmas season, for it prophesies the coming of our Savior, Jesus, some seven hundred years before the event happened. Yet look again and you may find there exactly what you need for today, for the verse contains four different names for our Lord.

Do you need wisdom and guidance today? He is your "Wonderful Counselor" who has all knowledge and sees the end from the beginning. Perhaps you need a big job done, something that *only* God can do. Remember that He is your "Mighty God," with all power in heaven and on earth.

Are you hurting and you need God's comfort? Isaiah says He is your "Everlasting Father." God is more attentive and loving than the best earthly father.

Is your heart in turmoil? Then you need the "Prince of Peace," who can bring the calmness you so desperately yearn for. Pour out your heart to Him. Let Him carry the weight of your concern. There is no peace so complete as what you will experience when you give the Lord your burden.

Friend, don't wait until a difficult situation drives you to call on God as your Wonderful Counselor, Mighty God, Everlasting Father, and Prince of Peace; turn to Him today.

88

"Be strong and courageous. Do not be afraid or terrified because of them, for the Lord your God goes with you; he will never leave you nor forsake you."

DEUTERONOMY 31:6

A RUSSIAN CHRISTMAS STORY

In 1994, two American teachers invited by the Russian government to teach biblical ethics visited an orphanage. It was Christmas, so the Americans gathered the abandoned and abused children together to tell them the story of the first Christmas.

Afterwards they gave the children pieces of cardboard to make a manger, tissue to tear into straw, flannel for a blanket, and a tiny baby cut from tan felt. The orphans busily assembled their mangers as the Americans walked around to offer help.

When one of the teachers came to where six-year-old Misha sat, she was startled to see not one but two babies in Misha's manger. Quickly, she called for the translator to ask why there were two. The boy repeated the Christmas story accurately—until he came to when Mary put baby Jesus in the manger. Then Misha related,

And when Mary laid the baby in the manger, Jesus looked at me and asked me if I had a place to stay. I told Him I have no mama and papa. Then Jesus told me I could stay with Him.

But I told Him I couldn't, because I didn't have a gift to give Him like everybody else. But I wanted to stay with Jesus so much. I thought maybe if I kept Him warm, that would be a good gift.

So I got into the manger, and then Jesus looked at me and He told me I could stay with Him—for always.

You too can have Jesus with you always. If you invite Him, you have His promise, "The LORD your God. . .will never leave you nor forsake you" (Deuteronomy 31:6).

89

*"On that day a fountain will be opened to the house
of David and the inhabitants of Jerusalem,
to cleanse them from sin and impurity."*

ZECHARIAH 13:1

THE FOUNTAIN THAT
WASHES AWAY GUILT

You've no doubt heard the saying, "Variety is the spice of life," but you may not know that it was written by a famous hymn-writer and poet named William Cowper.

Cowper lived a very troubled life. Suffering from severe depression, he repeatedly attempted to take his life. John Newton, composer of the hymn "Amazing Grace," became concerned with Cowper's increasing melancholy. Hoping to lift Cowper's spirits by keeping him busy, Newton suggested that he and Cowper co-author a book of 280 hymns, which they did.

After his first attack of deep depression, Cowper felt as if he had offended God so deeply that he could never be forgiven. Then Zechariah 13:1 spoke to his heart: "On that day a fountain will be opened to the house of David. . . to cleanse them from sin and impurity." Cowper realized God can erase the stain of any sin. From this experience he wrote one of his most famous hymns. The lyrics go:

There is a fountain filled with blood
drawn from Emmanuel's veins;
And sinners plunged beneath that flood
lose all their guilty stains.
The dying thief rejoiced to see
that fountain in his day;
And there have I, though vile as he,
washed all my sins away.

Cowper died in 1800. In Westminster Abbey, the first stained glass window on the left is an image of William Cowper. Under it is the title of his famous hymn, "There Is a Fountain Filled with Blood."

Cowper's life celebrated the apostle Paul's declaration that "All are justified freely. . .through the redemption that came by Christ Jesus. . .through the shedding of his blood—to be received by faith" (Romans 3:24–25).

90

This is love: not that we loved God, but that he loved us and sent his Son as an atoning sacrifice for our sins.

1 JOHN 4:10

THE DISCIPLE WHOM JESUS LOVED[1]

Five times in the New Testament, John is called "the disciple whom Jesus loved." Five times ought to be enough to convince anyone that Jesus really did love this man, right? What is interesting is that all five occur in one of the books John himself wrote, the Gospel of John. In other words, John described himself.

Did Jesus love him? Certainly He did; He loved all of His disciples. Do you think He loved John more than the other disciples? No, there is no indication of that in the Bible. So was it wrong for John to call himself the disciple whom Jesus loved? I don't think so. The only thing in which he boasted was the fact that Jesus loved him.

Jesus loved John—and He also loves you. Then aren't you too the disciple whom Jesus loves? Did you ever think of yourself as "the disciple whom Jesus loves"?

We know what love is because God first loved us. "This is love: not that we loved God, but that he loved us and sent his Son as an atoning sacrifice for our sins" (1 John 4:10).

Jesus died for us. That is how much He loves us! Karl Barth, the Swiss theologian, was asked about the most profound thing he had learned in his theological studies. He replied, "Jesus loves me, this I know, for the Bible tells me so."

The next time you stand in front of a mirror, look right into your own eyes and say, "I am the disciple whom Jesus loves." And then thank Him for that truth.

[1] I'm indebted to my dad, Dr. Guy Duffield, for this selection. These thoughts are from what people tell me was their favorite sermon he preached in his eighty-nine years.

WE WOULD LOVE TO HEAR FROM YOU!

Please share with us how this book has helped or blessed you. Or for additional needs, contact Darlene Sala at

Guidelines International Ministries
26161 Marguerite Parkway, Suite F,
Mission Viejo, California 92692

Or by email at
darlene@guidelines.org

MORE INSPIRATION FOR YOUR SOUL...

You Are Chosen

Bestselling author Darlene Sala inspires Christian women with these 90 encouraging readings. In *You Are Chosen*, readers will see God's desire for them, His determined choice to make them His daughters, and what He can accomplish through His grace.

Paperback / 978-1-68322-452-5 / $4.99

its a small town life!